POSITIVE PARENTHOOD

Other Books by Paul S. Graubard

CLASSROOMS THAT WORK
(with Harry Rosenberg)

A HANDBOOK OF BEHAVIOR MODIFICATION FOR THE CLASSROOM
(with Abraham Givner)

POSITIVE PARENTHOOD

SOLVING PARENT-CHILD CONFLICTS THROUGH BEHAVIOR MODIFICATION

BY

PAUL S. GRAUBARD

THE BOBBS-MERRILL COMPANY, INC.

INDIANAPOLIS / NEW YORK

Published by the Bobbs-Merrill Company, Inc.
Indianapolis New York

Designed by Jacques Chazaud
Manufactured in the United States of America

First printing

Library of Congress Cataloging in Publication Data

Graubard, Paul S.
Positive parenthood.

1. Children—Management. 2. Behavior modification.
3. Parent and child. I. Title.
HQ769.G735 649'.1 76–45574
ISBN 0–672–52240–3

Acknowledgments

I especially thank my wife Joy for her help with our children and for keeping things together when I was writing or staring into space. She spent many hours editing and reworking parts of the manuscript, and I appreciate it.

I also thank the parents and children I worked with, for they were my teachers as much as I was theirs. Many friends, neighbors and colleagues helped by criticizing portions of the book and by sharing their ideas and knowledge with me, especially Tilo Kaufmann, Kathy Arn, Joan Gross, Paul Lippmann, Ann and Jack Nolan, Cindy Taylor, Virginia Rowe, Joan Kaplan, Bob and Carolyn Boss, Dan and Susan O'Leary, Marty Gittelman, Jean Osborn, Susie Hamner, and Risa Graubard. Abe Givner and Helen Merrill were especially encouraging when I needed support. Diane Giddis, my editor, was a pleasure to work with.

Joel Curran, M.D., and Robert Taylor, M.D., gave the entire book a thorough professional reading, and I thank them.

I owe Michael, Risa, Amy and David Graubard a lot of time that I intend to make up to them.

P.S.G.

To Joy and our children—Risa, Amy, Michael and David

Contents

PREFACE *xi*

I. Behavior Modification—An Overview *1*

II. Increasing Desirable Behavior *9*

III. Decreasing Undesirable Behavior *30*

IV. Behavior Modification and Parents *43*

V. Eating *55*

VI. Toilet Training *77*

VII. Sleep and Nighttime Problems *91*

VIII. Fears *100*

IX. Schools *117*

X. Socialization *137*

XI. Social Problems *150*

XII. Responsibility and Independence *171*

AFTERWORD: You *183*

BIBLIOGRAPHY *185*

INDEX *187*

Preface

I was one of those husbands who thought that homemaking was a breeze. Being a homemaker, I imagined, would give me more time to be with my kids and to do a lot of other things I wanted to do as well. My job was getting routine, and the commuting more and more difficult to bear. My wife Joy and I talked about switching roles.

During the eighteen years I had worked, Joy had cleaned the toilet bowl at least 3,000 times, mopped the kitchen floor over 6,000 times, and fixed over 15,000 meals for me and our four children. She wanted a change too, for she was as tired of her work as I was of mine. We agreed to try the switch for one year. She took a teaching job and became the breadwinner. I turned to the task of keeping the house and raising the children.

My personal goals for the year were quite modest. I wanted, of course, to be an outstanding father. At the same time, I wanted to write a children's play, create one large or several small appliquéd wall hangings, become a superb French cook, and practice the guitar.

Disillusionment came fast. I had some outside household help, but even so there were days when everything simply fell apart. The work was endless. If I wasn't changing diapers I was cleaning house or washing clothes. Dust and clutter and dog hair began to fill the family room, toys and clothes inched their way up the stairs, and the dishes overflowed the sink.

The children turned out to be more work than I had ever imagined. If I didn't have much experience in being a househusband, I had even less in being a parent. A lot of what I did for the kids they should have done for themselves. When I wasn't settling fights, I was tying shoes or shopping. I changed the two-year-old's clothes three or four times a day, scrubbed hands and faces, did the laundry, set the table, cooked, washed dishes, and did everything else I thought four children required. I found I had even less time for myself than formerly. Joy helped me as much as she could, but she found—as I had—that earning a living and commuting left precious little time for homemaking.

The house had functioned well when my wife was in charge of things; I began to realize the price of that pleasant state. When Joy had said she never had a minute to breathe, she was understating the case. Everything had always gotten done, but she had done most of it. Frankly, I did not want to put that much work, or time, into running the house. Taking care of my family and being with them were my first priorities, but I wanted to get some personal work done too.

As slow a learner as I was, I eventually realized that there was a relationship between my lack of free time and my children's dependence. I began to demand that they do certain things for themselves and help around the house. They reacted with indifference or antagonism. The older ones' immediate retort was always, "That's not my job." The younger ones said, "Mommy always did it for me."

I grew concerned about my children's development. I knew they had to learn to take on greater responsibility in order to grow up. I had been aware that I would be expected to provide nurturing; it began to dawn on me how much teaching I would have to do as well.

Every child, at one time or another, has to be taught many things: what the bathroom is all about, how to tie shoes, how to dress, how to clean up after himself or herself, how to get along with people—the list could go on and on. Every child has to learn some much harder lessons as well—how to be independent, how to gain self-respect, how to get along with others.

Part of childhood has to do with preparing for adult life; at the same time, childhood—with its curiosity, discovery and awe—is a significant part of life itself. It deserves to be a happy and fulfilled time for everyone. I wanted to establish conditions that fostered both growth and the pleasures of childhood, and I was failing on both counts. I believed there had to be a better way.

I was grateful for the help I got from my wife, the cleaning woman, and Dr. Spock, but I needed more. I went to the library and looked through a score of books on raising children. Few of them were specific. What I could not find, and what I missed most, was a good "how-to-do-it" guide. I knew there were no magic formulas for raising children, but I wanted to learn some way of doing things that would make life easier for all of us.

I found that source in my own previous work. I am a child psychologist and a college professor. I had worked professionally with hundreds of families and thousands of children. My specialty was behavior modification; I had used it to help children overcome social and academic difficulties and learn new skills and attitudes, and to help families interact more effectively.

It is a well-known adage that the shoemaker's children often go without shoes. In like fashion, I had not previously applied my skills to important aspects of my own children's development—at least not in any systematic way. I had done the best I could to help with child-rearing and household tasks, but my career was demanding and I had been ambitious; I hadn't put in nearly as much time with the children as I should have. Now with my suddenly heightened concern about my children (not to mention my own survival needs), I began very consciously to apply behavior modification to the child-rearing problems that were overwhelming me.

During the year I was the "father of the house," I used behavior modification to toilet-train my youngest son in one day. I taught the others to fulfill their share of the household responsibilities (although that training is still going on). With my wife, I helped our eldest son overcome a serious reading disability. Together, we taught our two daughters to stop "borrowing" each other's clothes—this alone decreased the arguments between them by at least fifty percent.

At the same time, the children's self-confidence grew as they learned to do more things for themselves. We accomplished this in part by concentrating on what they could do—their achievements and successes—as opposed to their inadequacies. This helped our children learn positive attitudes. So did setting high standards and not doing for them what they could do for themselves.

My yelling and nagging declined dramatically, and eventually I found child-rearing to be the most gratifying part of my responsibilities. Because I got more work done, I had more time to be with and to take care of my family. In fact, we all had more time for the fun and sharing of family life.

Perhaps the success of the methods should not have surprised me, but it did. In my own professional work I had seen it used with remarkable effectiveness to help children overcome learning disabilities and to help troubled families resolve serious problems. Why shouldn't it work in families that are basically "normal" as well?

At the end of the year, my wife and I both admitted that we found our new roles and career changes disquieting. She felt displaced, and I felt economically dependent. The shift was too extreme for us. Now we both work part-time and share the breadwinning as well as the child care and the housework. But we continue to use behavior modification methods to solve family problems.

This book is the how-to-do-it guide that I, as a father, felt the need for. Although it was inspired by my experience with my children, it also draws on the work I have done with other families, before and since. The methods I describe are based on the principles of behavior modification. Behavior modification is only one way to work with children; it is neither the first nor the last word about the process of child-rearing. But it helped me. I believe it can also help you and your family as you face the day-to-day problems and crises involved in being a parent.

God could not be everywhere and so invented parents.

(adapted from an African folksaying)

CHAPTER I

Behavior Modification—An Overview

In Hebrew folklore a story is told about a teacher who wrote the letters of the alphabet on bread. Instead of ink he used honey. As the children learned the letters, they were allowed to eat the bread and honey. "This was done," the teacher said, "so that learning would be delicious." And that is what this book is all about—how to teach children what they need to learn in a way that is delicious. As a parent of four children, I can promise you it won't always be easy. Rough times as well as joyous ones are part of raising a family. But getting over the humps can be facilitated through behavior modification.

In the past ten years psychologists have discovered more about the principles of child behavior than they had in the one hundred years before that. The teaching method based on these principles—behavior modification—has been used with noteworthy success. With it psychologists and other professionals have helped children overcome nervous habits, fears, excessive shyness, and other problems. They have also employed it to enable children to master social and academic skills.

There is no reason why parents cannot take advantage of this method and apply it to their own child-rearing problems. Many psychologists have already taught parents how to use behavior modification methods to help their children conquer excessive fears, stop bedwetting, lose or gain weight, get along better with their brothers and sisters, and do better in school. Parents have also used the methods to help their children learn such skills as using a toilet, caring for their own rooms, putting dishes in the sink, hanging up clothes, establishing routines and observing good study habits.

The purpose of this book is to describe ways in which you as a parent can use behavior modification methods to help children learn such skills and to overcome behavior problems in the areas of eating, sleeping, toilet training, learning, social development, and personal responsibility. It also suggests ways to change your own behavior and set up family programs. It is meant to be a handbook; it is not a substitute for professional guidance. But it can aid you in getting over many of the difficulties one faces as a parent. The book stresses the mechanics of child-rearing, although it is understood that there is more to parenting than that.

What Is Behavior Modification?

Behavior modification is a method of consciously changing behavior by first identifying the behavior, then applying a consequence to that behavior. If you want to encourage the behavior, the consequence is known as "reinforcement." Think of it as a *when-then* proposition: *when* you see the desired behavior, *then* reinforce it. A reinforcer is a reward that works. A reinforcer will increase the number of times the behavior occurs.

Just as natural laws—like the law of gravity or the fact that heat rises—apply to our lives whether we are aware of them or not, so behavior follows certain laws or principles. These principles apply to parent–child relationships, even if we are not conscious of them. Every parent uses behavior modification in one form or another. Every time a parent communicates approval or disapproval to a child, the parent is attempting to modify the behavior of his or her child, even if the attempt is not successful. You might as well do it right.

Behavior modification sounds simple, and in many respects it is. To repeat: behavior that is reinforced will be strengthened; behavior that is not reinforced will be weakened. That is the essence of the method. Reward a child for the good things he or she does, and those good things are likely to be repeated. Conversely, if you do *not* reinforce behaviors, they are not likely to be repeated.

Psychologists have extended this common-sense approach into a three-step system:

1. *Identify* the behavior to be increased or decreased. (If the behavior is to be decreased, choose another behavior to take its place.)
2. *Intervene.* Reinforce the desired behavior.
3. *Evaluate.* Observe the results. (And, if necessary, try again.)

If you use the system correctly, you can help almost any child, regardless of age, to change almost any behavior. The step-by-step procedures to help children learn new ways of behaving are presented in the next chapter. Following are examples of how three different families used the three-step system to solve some common problems. The problems involve a preschooler, a child just entering school, and a teenager.

Joan Smith was three. She was a lovely child, but she had a bad habit: she fought a great deal on the playground. It was getting to the point where other parents kept their children away from her. Mrs. Smith knew she had to do something quickly, so she set up a behavior modification program for her daughter.

1. *Identify the behavior to be increased or decreased.* Fighting was the problem behavior, and clearly it had to be decreased. Mrs. Smith decided to increase cooperative play to take its place.

2. *Intervene.* Mrs. Smith told Joan that she was not permitted to fight because she could get hurt or could hurt someone else. Besides, the mother explained, children would not want to play with her if she fought with them.

Joan's mother told her she would help her overcome this habit. She instructed Joan to come to her if she encountered problems, and she and Joan would work out a peaceful solution. If she did fight, Joan was told, she would have to go home immediately. To reward her for not fighting (and to remind her as well), Mrs. Smith said she would give her a medal—a purple star printed on the back of her hand—for every fifteen minutes she went without fighting.

Joan loved the purple stars she earned. She also loved the praise and the attention her mother gave her—and even the advice she received on how to stay out of fights. The stars became even more valuable when her father, after counting the stars on her hand, complimented her on her achievements. He also made Jell-O with her because he was so proud of her and so pleased with the way she was helping herself. Joan strove for even more stars, because the experience of getting them was so pleasant.

3. *Evaluate.* Joan got into fewer and fewer fights. Not every day was perfect, by any means, but eventually she stopped fighting altogether. One day someone even complimented Mrs. Smith on how nicely her daughter played with the other children.

Now let's look at how the method can be used with a six-year-old.

Evan Austin was an eager and curious child, at times rambunctious, but hardly ever less than plain lovable—until he started to school. For some reason he resisted leaving the house in the morning. By the middle of the semester his misbehavior had escalated to the point of near mutiny. He woke up cross and irritable; he could never get out of bed until the fifth warning. Spankings and nagging didn't help. Evan's mother and father looked for clues to the cause of this difficulty, but nothing that Evan or his teacher said pointed to any specific reasons. The problem, whatever the reason, was clearly one for the home to solve.

1. *Identify the behavior to be increased or decreased.* The biggest problem the Austins faced was getting Evan off to school on time. In close order came having him eat breakfast, brush his teeth, wash up, and dress himself. Those were all behaviors they wanted to increase.

2. *Intervene.* Mr. Austin knew Evan loved to watch TV, so he decided to use television as the reinforcer in the plan he was devising. He cut up strips of cardboard and wrote down on each: "The holder of two of these tickets may watch the ——TV show." Then he made up more tickets and put the names and pictures of Evan's favorite snacks and games on them. He chose games that he knew Evan liked and that either of the parents could play.

Mr. Austin explained the plan very carefully to his son. In exchange for extra privileges, Mr. Austin told Evan, he had to get dressed, wash his face, brush his teeth, and be downstairs in a half hour. He would have to eat breakfast, clear his plate from the table, and be at the bus stop by ten minutes to eight.

Mr. Austin brought a digital clock to Evan's room to help him keep track of the time. He took great care to explain to Evan why he had to do those things and promised him that from now on he would no longer nag him. Evan earned one ticket for being downstairs, one ticket for eating and clearing his plate, and still another for being at the bus stop on time. He could exchange two tickets for a later than usual TV program and one ticket for a snack or an activity. Mr. Austin made it clear to Evan that if he didn't earn enough tickets, he could not watch TV past the usual time or have a snack or a game. In addition, Mr. Austin said that if Evan missed his bus he would just have to be late for school and then work that out with his teacher by himself.

Evan earned not a single ticket the first day. That evening he turned on the TV to watch a special program. No picture, no sound. His father held up the cord he had pulled out. "I'm sorry, Evan, but you didn't earn any tickets this morning, and I'm not going to let you watch a late program tonight," he said.

Evan tried to put the plug back in, but his father wouldn't allow it. Tears welled up in his eyes, and he begged for another chance. His father firmly told him that the only way he could watch late programs was by earning tickets. Again he explained to Evan how the system worked.

The next morning when the alarm went off, Evan bounced out of bed and got dressed. By the time he left for school, he had dressed himself, eaten a big breakfast, cleared his plate, brushed his teeth, and earned his three tickets.

Mr. Austin accompanied each ticket with a great deal of praise and many hugs. His praise was to the point. He did not say, "You're a good boy, Evan." He told him, "Evan, it's marvelous that you're out of bed so fast," or "You got dressed in six minutes this morning—I think that's wonderful." He used specific praise for specific behavior.

3. *Evaluate.* Mr. Austin noted that Evan had met his responsibilities every day. After one week he was tempted to drop the system, but he wanted Evan to develop good habits in this area, so he kept the system going for another two weeks. Then, when the habits were firmly established, he dropped it. Evan was still allowed to watch his programs, however, because mornings no longer presented a problem.

As a happy by-product, the Austins discovered that they now had more time to be with Evan in a loving and positive way. They found it fun to play the special games with him. Mr. Austin also felt a tremendous sense of accomplishment when he saw the changes that were taking place in Evan, especially when he remembered how only a few weeks before he had been screaming and nagging at his son constantly.

My daughter Amy was sixteen. She had just received her driver's permit and was ecstatic about it. But there were times when she was hard to live with. We would argue about her curfew and about the condition in which she left the kitchen. I wanted her last few years at home to be as pleasant as possible for everyone. Still, I didn't want her coming home at all hours of the night, and I didn't want to clean up after her.

1. *Identify the behaviors to be increased or decreased.* I wanted Amy to come home at ten-thirty on school nights, and I wanted her to clean up the kitchen when she was through with it.

2. *Intervene.* I made a deal with her. I would allow her to use the car on Saturday afternoons or Sundays, but she had to be responsible. Being responsible meant that she paid for her own gas, was home every school night before ten-thirty, and kept the kitchen clean. I was very specific about what I expected as far as cleaning up was concerned. Amy agreed. She wanted to use the car a great deal, and she knew that the only way she could get it was to live up to her part of the bargain.

3. *Evaluate.* Each night I checked to see whether Amy was home before ten-thirty and whether she had cleaned up any mess she had made in the kitchen. She came in every night before the designated time and the kitchen was always in order.

Benefits of Behavior Modification

All the parents in the preceding examples wanted to help their children, and themselves, as directly and economically as possible. They could have approached the problems in many ways. They could have waited for their children to outgrow them or they could have resigned themselves to their children's behavior. They could have consulted therapists or other experts. Instead they chose to act themselves. That's usually the easiest way to solve a problem.

The method they chose, behavior modification, is a direct one. It involves specifying what goals you will work toward. Because it is goal-oriented, it helps you to focus your thinking and to clarify the issues in a situation. And once you have pinpointed the goal, it is possible to keep track of whether or not you are proceeding toward it. Just knowing where you are going can be a big help, to adult and child alike.

Ideally, the child should want to work with you, for the outcome should be to his or her benefit or to the mutual benefit of you and your child. Instead of the will of the parent being forced on the child, both of you should approach the project as a joint one.

If you are willing to invest some time and energy in the behavior modification method, you can rest assured that it will be effective. It will be efficient, too. In today's busy world, efficiency is important. Child-rearing takes a lot of time, especially if you want to do it well. So does making a living, not to mention pursuing one's other interests. An efficient child-rearing method will allow you greater choice in how you spend your time.

There will of course be times when you make mistakes. Inconsistency and unnecessary punishment are the usual ones parents make. But since evaluation is part of the method, if and when problems come up you will always see what is happening. You will then know what to change. Evaluation eliminates a lot of guesswork. It minimizes the need for an expert. The facts are the facts.

Another benefit of the approach is that it can be used *anytime* during a child's development. Even if a problem erupts with an adolescent, or a habit has been present for a long time, it still can be changed with this method.

The term behavior modification sounds harsh, mechanical, and authoritarian to many people. It often conjures up images of drugs, mind control, and psychosurgery. These are not instances of behavior modification. Extreme forms of punishment are sometimes used in behavior modification, but only when a child is engaged in severely self-destructive behavior, such as self-mutilation. Even then punishment is used only when all other methods have failed. That is not the kind of behavior modification I will be discussing.

In fact, probably the best thing about the method is that it gives parents an alternative to punishment. Evan's parents had used punishment—with little effect. Behavior modification encourages a child to act positively, because you set a positive example. And the child reacts positively to the appreciation he or she receives. Everyone likes to be complimented and rewarded for doing a good job, and children are no exception.

We should, in fact, continually look for and encourage appropriate behavior in our children. Sometimes we find it much easier to be critical than to see and talk about their strengths. We need to tell them how marvelous they are and *why* we think so. Love and affection, felt and expressed honestly, encourage behavior that leads to growth. Loving our children for who they *are,* and not for what we think they *should* be, also fosters feelings of competence and self-worth.

Often, in fact, by focusing on a child's misbehavior we strengthen it. Many children discover that more attention is paid to their bad behavior than to their good behavior. ("Good" and "bad" in this book are not meant in any moral sense; rather, they refer to behaviors that you would like to increase and decrease, respectively). With this discovery, the script starts to write itself: more misbehavior. Some parents inadvertently encourage their children to take up a pattern of negative behavior by behaving in a negative way themselves, lavishing shouts and threats and other signs of disapproval on them. Any attention is better than none; when the major attention parents pay to their children is some form of disapproval, children tend to see themselves as "bad" and to act accordingly. Behavior modification, along with regular displays of affection and encouragement, can save many parents from falling into this all too common trap.

This is not to imply that behavior which parents find objectionable only comes about because a child learns that he or she has to be "bad" to get attention. Misbehaving, if you will remember, can be fun, and sometimes it seems easier to break the rules than to follow them. Often children are not even aware of what behavior is acceptable and what behavior is objectionable. The point is that if children are encouraged to behave appropriately, they will find "good" behavior more rewarding than "bad" behavior in the long run.

The cornerstone of behavior modification is the premise that rewards and praise are much more effective than punishment. Reward is therefore the predominat feature of behavior modification that I will be discussing. In the chapters that follow, you will find detailed descriptions of behavior modification techniques as well as prescriptions for their use.

CHAPTER II

Increasing Desirable Behavior

This chapter describes how to use behavior modification. After you learn the principles, you can apply them creatively, adapting them to your individual situation. You will be able to prevent problems as well as remedy them. Let's discuss more fully the three basic steps.

Step One: Identify the Problem Behavior(s)

First identify what the child does that makes up the problem. Johnny *hits* Billy. Mary *cries* nineteen times a day. Johnny *crawls out* of his crib at night. Behavior is simply an observable action—something somebody does. Behaviors can be observed and counted; whether a particular behavior has or has not taken place is subject to little interpretation. Behavior is *not* an unseen thing that occurs inside someone. It is *not* an attitude or a feeling, as important as attitudes and feelings might be. Changing the way a person behaves usually changes the way he or she feels, but you need to concentrate on behavior to change the feeling. Behavior is something you can actually see. The more precise you are in identifying what behaviors you want to change, the easier the method is to use.

The Austins wanted Evan to be *washed up, dressed, fed,* and *outside in time* to catch the school bus. I wanted Amy to be *home at a specific time* and to *clean up after herself.* These are specific behaviors that were pinpointed for change. Their very specificity accounted in large part for the improvement that resulted.

Here are some examples of specific behaviors, both desirable and undesirable:

sweeping the floor	throwing a jacket on the floor
eating vegetables	leaving dirty dishes on the table
smiling	fighting
drinking milk	playing with electrical outlets

All these are behaviors you can see and count. They either occur or don't occur.

Here are some non-specific descriptions:

being a good girl	being lazy
being cooperative	being bad
being polite	being hyperactive
having a good attitude	having a bad attitude

Saying a child is lazy is not being specific. You can't count laziness. Your own definition of laziness might vary from day to day. Your mood might determine what you consider to be lazy. A term such as "lazy" doesn't tell you where to begin tackling the problem, because you don't know specifically which behaviors have to be increased so that a child won't be considered lazy anymore. Descriptions such as "rude," "hyperactive," or "has a poor attitude" can tell you a lot about a person generally, but they do not supply information to map out a specific program.

To plan a specific program, it is necessary to break up general terms, such as "lazy," into specific behaviors. Ask yourself what the child does or doesn't do that makes you consider him or her lazy. Does he leave his room in a mess in the morning? Does she fail to make the bed? Are the peanut butter and the jelly left on the kitchen counter after an afternoon snack? Do you have to call him three times before he answers? Does she fail to complete her chores? All of these are specific behaviors you can observe. You can count how many times the peanut butter and the jelly are left out. The more specifically you define a behavior, the easier it will be to change it, because you will have a precise and consistent target to aim at. You can do something about each one of these behaviors—not all at once, of course, but you'll know where to begin.

Until you have pinpointed the behavior you wish to alter, it is impossible to communicate your expectations to the child or to yourself. Without a specific destination, you won't even know in which direction to move—let alone how to get there.

For example, one mother asked a psychologist for advice on how to get her daughter to "respect" her. When asked what she meant, the woman was unable to define the term. It took the psychologist a good half hour to find out finally that to this mother "respect" meant that her daughter should clean up after herself, help with meals, and stop mimicking and making smart-alecky remarks. Once the mother had pinpointed the specific behaviors, the psychologist was able to help her. "Respect" is a term that can cover a variety of behaviors: it can mean smiling, making pleasant rather than snide remarks, kissing the parents good night, doing the dishes, setting the table, shutting doors quietly, and so forth. These are all observable behaviors. It is up to you to decide if one, two, all or none of these represent your idea of "respect."

What behaviors should a parent pick to increase or decrease? That all depends on the child's needs—and on yours. Behavior modification can tell you *how* to teach, but not *what* to teach. Most parents, however, have little trouble deciding on what is important for their children to learn. Parents usually know best what their children should or should not do.

Objectivity and detachment are helpful in deciding what it is important to work on. If you feel you've lost perspective, pretend you're thinking about someone else's child. List some of the problems that are bothering the family. It's best to do this when the children are asleep and you're in a mellow mood. List only behaviors—what the child does or doesn't do. It is also a good idea to write down some of the child's strengths. That kind of perspective helps you feel better about the child and can add to your confidence and satisfaction over the job you've already done.

From the problem behaviors you have listed, cross out those that aren't really important and those that can be responsibly ignored. Choose just one or two things that could help the child (and family) if they were changed for the better. You can get to the others later.

Now ask yourself a hard question. Why do you want to change the behavior? (Or, whose problem is it?) There are lots of things that children do or don't do that won't be problems to them if they're not problems to you. Disliking sports, wearing long hair, and reading comic books instead of Shakespeare are some examples. It makes no difference in the long run whether or not a child likes to play baseball. To get him to participate in something he finds distasteful is a waste of energy for both of you. There is nothing wrong with encouraging a child to try new things, but children are surely just as entitled to their likes and dislikes as adults are.

Some of the things a child might like to do—listen to a radio at high volume, for example—are more problematic. Your child has rights, but so do you. Problems in which one person's rights begin to infringe on another's are usually best solved through discussion and compromise rather than explicit reinforcement systems. Sensitivity is needed to resolve such problems, and a child best learns sensitivity through example and encouragement.

Leaving a mess in the kitchen, being rude, and failing to master toilet skills are behaviors that a parent should change. They violate your rights and will be harmful to the child in the long run unless they're corrected.

So, when selecting a behavior for change, be sure you can justify it as being for the good of the child or for your mutual good. If you cannot justify what you are doing, it makes more sense to leave it alone and tackle other problems instead.

If you're satisfied with the behaviors you have chosen and they need to be increased, you've already completed the first step. If you've decided that the behaviors need to be decreased, there's still one more step to go.

That step is picking a behavior to take the place of the one you want to decrease. Behavioral psychologists often use the term *fair-pair* to describe reinforcing one behavior sufficiently to take precedence over another. For example, getting David to stop throwing his books on the floor is only part of the problem, exasperating as that might be. If you get him to put the books on the shelf, he can't put the books on the floor. Setting up fair-pairs is more effective, more positive and easier than just discouraging the misbehavior. Behavior modification generally requires increasing behavior—often the opposite of what you want to decrease.

So, when you think of a negative behavior, think of what it takes to correct it. For example, if Johnny's leaving dishes in the sink is targeted for decrease, having him wash the dishes is the behavior that needs to be increased. If Kim hardly talks, you need to encourage her to participate in conversations. Here are a few more examples of fair-pairs:

wets diaper	uses toilet appropriately
leaves underwear on floor	puts underwear in hamper
shouts	talks quietly

Use positive thinking. The thought and feeling "I can't stand it when he/she does——" is at the heart of many parent–child problems. Often, too, the more you dislike a particular thing about yourself, the more you dislike what your child does in that area. (What to do with this feeling is discussed in Chapter 4.)

By now you should be able to list the behavior(s) you want to increase as well as the behavior(s) you want to decrease. If you're having trouble listing behaviors that are specific and observable or making fair-pairs, re-read this section. It is essential for effecting changes.

Step Two: Intervene

Now that you've identified the problem behavior, try to analyze why it is occurring. If there is a lot of fighting between brothers and sisters, ask yourself if one child (or all of them) is making a bid for attention in the only way he or she knows how. Do they have enough activities to keep them amused on those long winter nights? If there's a lot of bickering before dinnertime, would the situation be improved if the dinner hour were a little earlier or the children were fed separately? Could Johnny's reluctance to go to school be helped by having him tutored in math? Could Mary's tantrums be related to the fact that she thinks you were arbitrary and belittling in setting down restrictions? The more you can ascertain the motivation behind a child's behavior (granted, this is not always possible), the easier it will be to help the child.

In addition, look at the larger picture. Are you giving too little attention to your child? Does he need more structure in his life, or less? Are your expectations of him unrealistic? Is she depressed over an older sibling's treatment? An unhappy family situation, such as a divorce or the death of a loved one, will necessarily affect your child's behavior. So will tension or friction between the parents, or occupational problems requiring one or both parents' attention. If the problem seems to be tied to an adverse period in the family's life, you can probably weather it with love and understanding. But if it's a persistent or unusually disturbing one, you might want to consider professional help. I would suggest, however, that you try the system first; you have nothing to lose, and you might be surprised by what you gain.

Tutoring or changing the dinner hour can be very important, but first you have to know what the problem is. You can start the ball rolling in this area by talking *with,* not to, your child. Tell her what you feel. Ask her to do the same. See if the child has any suggestions for solving the problem. Share what you intend to do to improve the situation and why you are going to do it. It's always easier to work *with* someone than *on* him.

After you have identified and analyzed the problem—and made whatever changes were necessary to improve the situation—the next step is to reinforce the behavior you want to increase. This is where Grandma's Law comes in.

When–Then or Grandma's Law

Grandma's Law says simply, "You may have your ice cream after you have eaten your spinach." It is an ancient formulation of the when-then principle. It sums up one of the most important guides of child-rearing. *When* you incorporate this principle (consciously or unconsciously) into mothering or fathering, *then* you will find your task easier and your children more fun. What are the problems—toilet training, learning to dress himself, learning to clean up after herself, getting along with others, or one of the host of life-mastering skills he needs to learn as he grows up? *When* a child gets into her pajamas—*then* she can hear a story. *When* a child does her Saturday chores—*then* she can go out and play. Keep in mind the when-then principle in the course of bringing up your child. It is the nutrient that helps children grow.

The Gianelli family had two sons, Michael, eight, and David, six. Michael and David loved to eat. That pleased Mrs. Gianelli, but what galled her was that her children left their plates on the table and didn't put food back in the refrigerator. She spoke to them about it, appealed to their fairness, scolded them and even punished them. Their reform never lasted more than a day or two. She was getting more and more exasperated when an idea came to her.

The oldest son played in Little League; the youngest aspired to. She had once taken them to the Batting Cage, a concession where, for twenty-five cents, a machine pitched baseballs over the plate to a batter. The boys loved it and pestered their mother to take them there again.

She again spoke to them about the cleaning-up problem and asked for their cooperation. She told the boys that *when* they kept the kitchen neat for three days in a row, *then* she would take them to the Batting Cage. Each day she checked off whether they had cleaned up after themselves. Whenever she put down a check mark, or whenever she saw them straightening up, she thanked and complimented them. She also went out of her way to set a good example.

The boys did what they were asked to do without any trouble, and on the third day she took them to the Batting Cage. Mrs. Gianelli then required the boys to keep the kitchen clean for a week in exchange for another trip there. By this time, cleaning up after themselves was becoming a habit. Mrs. Gianelli continued to take them to the Batting Cage on occasion because they liked it so much and because she appreciated the change in their behavior.

Reinforcers

A reinforcer is anything that increases behavior. You use reinforcers all the time. When you clap your hands at your toddler's first steps, you expect your show of pleasure to encourage him to try again. And you're right; it does. When you tell your teenage daughter that her hair looks pretty, it encourages her to groom it. Intangible reinforcers can be just as powerful as tangible ones—often more so. Praise, a well-turned compliment, a hug or a kiss, a special smile, or a look of quiet approval can mean as much to a child as a treat or a TV show or a toy. And gestures of approval are practically limitless.

Your interest and encouragement are probably the greatest reinforcers of them all. You should not limit use of them to those times when you are trying to change behavior. Often children will spontaneously clean house, draw pictures, make things, or practice skills they learned in school. Take the time to notice those things and let the child know how proud and pleased you are—not only as their parent, but because they are learning and having fun. The chances are they will do more of the kinds of things both of you find pleasing.

Sometimes praise and encouragement do not come naturally or spontaneously. Then you have to invoke them deliberately. Make a concerted effort to find a certain number of things a day to praise.

Some parents find it quite helpful to keep a chart of their praising.

Every time they praise, they simply put an X in the box. The chart makes them conscious of how much or how little they express their appreciation. The chart could look like this:

M	T	W	Th	F	S	Sun
X	X	X				
X	X	X				
X	X	X				
X	X					
X	X					

Praise also needs to be very strong on occasion. I am not suggesting, though, that you be phony about praise. Children can usually detect that and resent it fiercely. Just try to build on your already existing feelings so that your delight and enthusiasm become apparent and contagious.

It is true that with some children great care must be exercised in giving praise or compliments. Such a child feels that the adult's praise establishes a standard he cannot live up to. If a child rejects praise and compliments, make what you say specific and factual. Instead of telling a child she is a good speller, note that she got seventeen out of twenty spelling words right. The former is a judgment with which the child might disagree. The latter is indisputable. When a child's confidence in her spelling increases, she'll be able to accept general compliments more readily. In the meantime just let her know you're aware of any improvements she's made.

Praise and verbal encouragement won't work miracles, however; sometimes a more concrete incentive is required. Michael and David Gianelli's habits in the kitchen could not be changed by praise alone; only specific reinforcement coupled with praise helped. Material reinforcers can be used effectively to alter difficult and well-established problem behaviors when everything else has failed.

Material reinforcers can be quite simple; they don't have to be expensive by any means. They can be such things as baseball cards, a miniature-golf game or dinner at Kentucky Fried Chicken.

One might ask why you should have to reinforce children for what they should do. The answer is that through reinforcement they will learn how to do it. The point is really to get the child to read or to clean up. If it takes reinforcement to do that, why not? Most of us have worked hard at some point to get something special, such as money for a vacation, free time to paint the picture we wanted to work on, and so forth. What's wrong with doing that for children too?

Reinforcing is not bribing. It is using an incentive to encourage good habits, habits that will eventually carry their own rewards. The incentive helps to get the habit started. Once a skill or habit has been established, the child's own self-esteem and your approval are the "natural" reinforcers for sustaining that skill. Many subtle influences work to maintain it: the recognition and respect of teachers, friends, brothers and sisters, the sense of belonging and of competency. Many skills also provide inherent pleasures, such as the joy of reading a good book (or looking up a TV schedule) once reading skills have been mastered. "Artificial" reinforcements such as points or toys or games need only be used as a bridge to learning new and difficult behaviors.

Nor is reinforcing manipulative. Mrs. Gianelli was quite straightforward in telling the boys why she was requiring them to clean up after themselves and why it was in everyone's best interest for them to do so.

The following reinforcers have proven effective:

- hugging and kissing
- clapping your hands
- playing Ring-around-the-Rosy
- smiling
- telling a story
- going for a walk
- taking trips to the park
- going sleigh-riding or swimming
- teaching a child how to ride a bicycle
- expressing praise and encouragement
- spending time alone with a child
- going fishing
- playing catch
- playing cards
- playing Monopoly or checkers
- promising to cut down on number of cigarettes you smoke
- playing miniature golf
- giving a child a driving lesson

Privileges

- the right to choose TV programs over a specific time period
- use of the family adding machine or typewriter
- use of the car

a later bedtime
extra TV time
sitting in the front seat of the car
permission to invite a friend over for dinner

Material

toys
sports equipment
lessons (music, dance, etc.)
a dollhouse or treehouse
little cars and soldiers
tools
scouting equipment

Food

popcorn
a favorite food for dinner
candy
raisins and nuts
sugarless bubble gum
an extra dessert
dinner at a hamburger place
a McDonald's gift certificate

Reinforcers Are Idiosyncratic

Not all of the preceding rewards would be helpful with all children. Some children couldn't care less about a fishing trip; some children would do almost anything to go. Everyone has particular tastes and likes and dislikes. That's why ice cream comes in different flavors.

Rewards or reinforcers must be wanted by a child if they are to be effective in motivating him or her. The best and *only* judge of what an effective reward might be is the child himself. If the reward does not increase the target behavior, it is not a reinforcer. If a child will not do what is required to get the reward, hold the reward in suspicion. You may have to increase the strength of the reward or switch to another one.

Careful looking and listening will tell you what a child wants. What does he do with his free time? What are his interests? Her favorite activities? When you go to the supermarket, what does she want? What does he always ask for, eat, do, dream about? It could be a snorkel or having the chain put back on a bike. It could be cookies or a chance to fly kites with her father. Whatever it is, if it is acceptable to you, follow your child's lead. Here is where your understanding of and empathy with your child come in. The more you are aware of your child's individuality, the more accurate you will be in choosing the right reinforcer for the purpose. And with a specific goal in mind, you will become more observant of a child's likes and dislikes.

Whenever possible, let a child participate in choosing a reward. Let him know what is required to earn it, and discuss what you each consider reasonable. Participation will give children an added interest in and commitment to completing their part of the bargain. And that helps both of you.

A note of caution: in selecting a reinforcer, try to avoid things that a child already has or should have. Exercise judgment in determining what is or is not a fair reinforcer.

When you have found an effective reinforcer, be careful not to overuse it. Children, like adults, get tired of the same thing all the time. They will reach the point where the motivator no longer works if it is used over and over again. Billy Gerber's father wanted his son to learn to read. He started using baseball cards as reinforcers. Once Billy had a complete collection of the Boston Red Sox, the cards no longer interested him. Mr. Gerber said that Billy could have a cap pistol when he learned a new list of words. The new reward worked.

Sometimes you can "create" a reinforcer—that is, allow the child to try something new, such as horseback riding, which will then provide motivation for him or her to change. This can be especially effective with a child who bores easily or is unusually energetic. Just remember not to force the child into the new activity.

Reinforce Immediately

Whatever the reinforcer, the relationship between the reward and the desired behavior must be direct and clear. One reason you should reinforce immediately is that in the child's mind it ties the reward to the behavior. In addition, the quickest way to establish a behavior is to reinforce it immediately. The moment a child finishes a task, express appreciation. As soon as your daughter has made her bed and picked up her socks and underwear, reward her with a hug and kiss, a snack of peanut butter and jelly, or whatever else you agreed upon or think will strengthen her interest in taking care of herself. When Evan came downstairs on time, his father immediately handed him a TV ticket and coupled it with praise; when Joan played for a while without fighting, she was given a medal on the back of her hand, as well as praise from her mother. The immediate experience of satisfaction or gratification is the fuel that powers the drive toward growth.

Don't interfere with this process by dragging your feet in delivering a well-earned reinforcer. After skills have been mastered, you can work on "delayed gratification" by letting a child choose a small reward now or a larger reward later. You can also require more work for the reward, just as Mrs. Gianelli did. It takes trial and error to find the balance, but it can be done.

For the reinforcer to work you have to set the requirements within easy reach. As meeting the goals becomes easier, set them a little higher. Mrs. Gianelli used that technique quite well when she first required her children to keep the kitchen clean for three days, and later, when the children could do that readily, for seven days. If she had told them they had to keep the kitchen clean for a month, it might not have been worth it to the children, and the good habits woudn't have been started.

The Idea Is to Make Success Inevitable

Some children can work hard on problem behaviors for long periods of time if the reinforcer is powerful enough. Other children do better with small rewards, such as a bag of chips or a toy soldier, given daily. Young children almost always need to be rewarded often to speed up the learning process. Older children can work toward longer-range goals, but here too they should receive positive feedback, such as points, which later can be exchanged for the reinforcer. (A point system works best with three-year-olds and up.)

Reinforce All Steps That Lead to the Goal

Some goals are too complex to reach all at once; you have to get there one step at a time. Take cleaning a room, for example. You cannot realistically expect a three-year-old with a history of leaving clothes and toys all over the room to change overnight because you have decided he is old enough to clean up after himself. Expecting too much too soon can only lead to power struggles, negativism and feelings of inadequacy.

A child first has to learn how to clean. You might start by teaching her to put away her toys. Emphasize how helpful the toy shelves or toy box can be to her. She'll always be able to find what she needs if it's in the right place. She won't trip over things or have to walk around them if they're put away neatly.

When she puts away a toy, immediately reward her. A kiss and a hug or a great big "Wonderful!" would do. At first you'll probably have to model the behavior you expect. Put a few toys on the shelf; then enlist her aid by having her hand you the toys. Then reverse your jobs: hand her the toys and let her put them away. Each time you should do less and allow her to do more until she can do the job all by herself. Once again, be sure to praise her and reward her with a story or a special game.

Then concentrate on hanging up clothes; when that has been mastered, go on to making the bed.

You can break any complex goal into specific parts by asking yourself what a person has to do to dress herself, clean a room, act politely, or whatever. Step by step, go through cleaning a room or riding a bicycle. Make believe you're doing those things. Write down each specific thing you have to do. If making a bed is too complex for a child, go through, in your imagination, all the things you do to make a bed—put on the bottom sheet by tucking one corner under the mattress, and then another, until you wind up putting on the bedspread.

Breaking complex goals into specific targets is also gratifying to an adult. Not only does it enable you to teach effectively, it allows you to see progress from your efforts, and you need that almost as much as the child does.

Reinforcement from Other Sources

Very often children are reinforced for negative behavior. This reinforcement (usually attention) can come from friends, brothers and sisters, or teachers, as well as from you. Instruct everyone that the most effective approach is to pay a lot more attention to positive behavior than to negative behavior. If necessary, reinforce the other children for ignoring the child's misbehavior or increase the strength of the original reward to overcome the influence of the other children.

Agreements and Contracts

In using behavior modification it is important to communicate specifically *what* the reward will be and *when* it will be given to the child. If an allowance is to be earned, the youngster needs to know what he has to do to earn the money, and the time and place he will receive payment. If he earns extra TV time, let your child know specifically what "extra" time means and how long he can use his privileges, just as Mr. Austin did with Evan.

Some families follow the practice of specifying agreements in writing. Putting it in writing is an excellent way of avoiding confusion and misunderstanding. A child can then see in black and white exactly what is expected, what the reward will be and when it will be given. If he can't read, at least he'll understand the importance of the printed page, and you'll have a record of what you said.

A contract has to possess at least three elements: (1) what the child is to do—quality as well as quantity needs to be spelled out; (2) what the adult will do—what kind of reinforcement will be provided and when it will be given (make directions clear); (3) exactly how the contract is to be monitored, by whom and when.

Two other aspects are optional: (4) sanctions—loss of TV time or recess if the contract is not lived up to and (5) bonuses for exceeding the requirements.

One set of parents worked out the following contract for their daughter regarding Friday dance lessons. It worked wonders in helping Melody through a hard thirteenth year.

Date ____________

Contract No. ________

I, Melody Jones, may earn the price of my dancing lesson by handing in my homework each day in Earth Science. To pick up my money I need to take a note from my science teacher to the office each week. If my teacher notes that I have handed in all of my assignments, the secretary will give me the envelope my parents dropped off. If I have not handed in my assignments, it is understood I will not receive the money for my dance lesson.

I, Melody Jones, agree to the terms of the agreement as stated above.

____

Melody Jones

We, the undersigned, agree to the terms of the contract as stated above.

Mr. Jones ____________ Mrs. Jones ____________

It is understood this contract expires in twelve weeks, at which time a new contract will be negotiated.

A "communication center" is a fine idea for busy families. The refrigerator can often serve that purpose, with schedules, messages, checklists of chores to be done, agreements, and points that can accumulate for special rewards attached to the door and sides. Many families prefer blackboards or bulletin boards. These are ways of organizing family life so that everyone can be aware of his responsibilities without the irritant of constant nagging or reminding. People also experience a sense of accomplishment when tasks are completed and crossed off a checklist. That is often a strong reinforcer in itself.

Delivering the Goods

Once an agreement is made, *the adult is honor bound to deliver as promised.* Sometimes there will be extenuating circumstances, but it must be made clear that this system will succeed only if commitments are kept. If you cannot keep them, explain why promptly and give a raincheck. But such arrangements and substitutions, if overdone, are likely to create a credibility gap that could be disastrous.

Learn to give reinforcers as quickly and as naturally as you can. For example, Chris ran into the house one sunny afternoon and took some watermelon out of the refrigerator. He asked his father to cut him a piece. His father cut the watermelon and told Chris he could have it when he had washed his hands and put back the uncut portion. The watermelon satisfied Chris and served to teach him to wash his hands before eating.

Sometimes it is hard for certain kinds of people to "deliver the goods" simply and straightforwardly. If you are one of these people, make extra efforts to keep your rewards as simple as possible, because rest assured that this method will not work if you cannot control your tendency to "mess up" agreements. You can also have the "goods" ready ahead of time. It is usually more motivating to a child anyway to see what she's getting, and it will help you to be prompt about delivering the reward.

Routines

A lot of problems will fade away as routines are established. When you've been successful in building the desired behavior, such as clearing the table after a meal, keep on working at it until it becomes a habit. Routines are to children what a foundation is to a house. Once you have a routine or a foundation, you can add onto it. Without a routine you have haphazardness and accident—and inordinate struggles to get to places on time, have clothes available, and accomplish the smallest task.

Once a routine has been established, problems with baths, meals and so forth will be cut in half. The child will know what is expected of him or her, and will gradually meet those expectations. If you take the time to think out the requirements for a well-run house, you will find it much easier to fulfill those requirements. Your child will also benefit immensely from the sense of order that will follow. Remember, however, to build time alone and time for fun into routines.

Consistency

Being consistent and systematic is perhaps the cardinal principle of child-rearing. If a mother refuses to grant a child's wishes, some children will go to the father with the same request, and vice versa. Children should understand that they cannot play off one parent against the other.

Children—and adults too, for that matter—like to know where they stand and what the consequences of their actions will be. Allowing your child to leave his clothes in a heap on the floor on Monday but punishing him for this same behavior on Tuesday will make him pay more attention to your mood than to the rules. His behavior will become like yours—arbitrary and erratic. If you are consistent in your behavior—whether you are reinforcing, ignoring or punishing—you will be able to teach more effectively. Being consistent is admittedly one of the most difficult standards to measure up to, but it is essential for effective child management. Part of being consistent is giving consequences a chance to work.

Modeling, or "Monkey See Monkey Do"

A difficult guideline to follow in parenting is to present a model of the behavior you wish your child to follow. Children learn by example. They will almost always do what you do, and not what you say should be done. If you want your children to speak in low voices, have agreeable manners, keep themselves and their rooms neat and clean and have good work habits, then set them an example by speaking in a low voice, having agreeable manners, and so forth. A parent who shouts or curses or smokes will find invariably that he or she has a houseful of children who shout, swear inordinately and develop the nicotine habit. And they will continue to swear no matter how many times you shout, "If there's anything I can't stand, goddammit, it's to hear a kid swear."

The Barretts decided to make house and yard chores a family project for Saturdays; everyone agreed to do his part. Father was a super organizer and delegator of responsibilities; however, when Saturday rolled around, he somehow always had at least three other important matters, deadlines and such, that required his immediate attention and precluded his participation in the clean-up sessions. Not surprisingly, the kids lost interest in the project and did sloppy jobs. Despite all of the yelling and cajoling from their parents, the children reached the point where they also found they had other more important tasks to do on Saturdays. (And here was a case where simple rewards wouldn't work either, because it had been set up as a family project, and the sense of teamwork and being together was the natural reinforcer that would have kept things going.) It wasn't until the father modeled the behavior he expected from his children—became a full partner in the cleaning too—that he was able to get the children to participate in the chores. The clean-up sessions then gave the family a valuable sense of partnership and closeness.

Parents who wish to generate non-sexist attitudes in their children must be aware of the importance of modeling in this area too: mothers can take over some of the responsibilities usually delegated to fathers, and vice versa. For instance, mothers might run the lawnmower or fix a light, while fathers might do some cooking or cleaning.

As a child learns new skills, he or she should be given new freedoms. These freedoms, because they have been earned, will lead to a sense of responsibility, as well as to feelings of competence and trust. When a child learns how to care for furniture, she should be allowed to sit in the living room. When a child learns to stop and look both ways, she should be allowed to cross the street by herself. If you have communicated praise and love, eventually habits and freedom will be all the reward that is necessary.

An important thing to remember when using behavior modification is to spend time with your child even when you are not teaching or changing behavior. Children are to be enjoyed, and just being with them is part of that enjoyment. If you are working with a child who needs particular help, spend time with him or her in other than a teaching way. Also, arrange times alone for the others. You don't want to give your children the idea that to get your interest and attention they need to have problems.

The tone of your voice and the attitude you convey are important parts of a behavior modification program. Reinforcers work best as an encouragement to children. If you threaten a child with not receiving a reward—or have to keep reminding him to work for it—you are in a power struggle. The best way to get out of that is just to walk away from it.

You should now be able to specify what behavior to increase and should know how to carry out an intervention program. The next section will tell you how to be sure you are on the right track.

Step Three: Evaluate

Keep a record of what happens. Records are at the very heart of behavior modification and the key to its accomplishments. Keep in mind that any behavior that can be counted can be changed. Monitoring your results will ensure success. Maybe the first program you start won't be the answer, but eventually you'll find the right one.

Keep records in the simplest possible way. Mrs. Gianelli just tacked a form on the bulletin board. It looked like this:

Table cleaned:	M	T	W	Th
	(Yes) No	(Yes) No	(Yes) No	(Yes) No

It served as a reminder to the children and to herself of what had to be done. It let her know whether the requirements were met and when it was time to give the reinforcer. It let the children know the same things.

An effective record tells you how many times the target behavior occurs. It should make clear whether there was an increase or decrease in the target behavior. All you need in the way of equipment is a pencil and paper. If your record-keeping system is complicated or time consuming, it will break down, so make it easy on yourself. You might also consider keeping the record in red. That way what's happening is quite apparent.

Let's look at how some families have monitored their plans. One family wanted to decrease fighting and increase cooperative play. The intervention they used was to tie going to the movies to five days of cooperative play. At the end of each day the father made the following entry, and everybody knew where he stood.

Cooperated with each other:	M	T	W	Th	F	S
	(Y) N	(Y) N	Y (N)	Y (N)	(Y) N	(Y) N

Another family tied a camping trip to a reduction in the number of fights each day. The deal was that when the children fought less each day for five days, they would go away the following weekend.

<table>
<tr><td>No. of fights:</td><td>M</td><td>T</td><td>W</td><td>Th</td><td>F</td><td>S</td></tr>
<tr><td></td><td>卌
||||
9</td><td>卌
||
7</td><td>卌
|
6</td><td>||||

4</td><td>0</td><td>0</td></tr>
</table>

Another family was concerned about clothes left on the floor and the amount of nagging the parent did. A reinforcer for both the parent and the child was tied to each getting down to 0. They monitored it with the following form.

	M	T	W	Th	F	S
Items left on floor:	4	3	4	2	1	0
Parent nags:	7	5	9	5	3	0

Another way to keep records is to list jobs (and standards if necessary), and then check off whether they were completed or not.

Keeping Track of Jobs

	M	T	W	Th	F
Make bed					
Stack dishes					
Clean lawn					
Walk dog					

Y = Yes; N = No.

Many parents have found the following form to be very effective in organizing a program:

1. Specify.
   I (we) want to increase ______________________________
   I (we) want to decrease ______________________________

2. Intervene. (Tell what you're going to do and what the child is expected to do [when-then].)

3. Evaluate.

One note about this formal method: it should not be used for every minor difficulty that comes up in child-rearing. You should reserve it for problems that disrupt the family or situations crucial to a child's development. Simply using when-then will help with most other problems.

At this point you should know how to (1) select a behavior for increase, (2) make up a reinforcement program, and (3) monitor your plan. Sometimes your plan will fail. Don't give up; you just have to work harder. The following checklist can help you spot where you've gone wrong.

1. Is your goal justified?
2. Is your goal specific?
3. Are there situational problems that can be corrected? When children get hungry or tired, they get cranky. Fighting can often be de-

creased by moving supper ahead or giving a snack (following good behavior, of course).

4. Have you been explicit about what the reinforcer is, when you will give it, and under what conditions?

5. Is the reinforcer truly something the child wants?

6. Is the reinforcement given immediately?

7. Are you requiring too large a step for the child to accomplish at present?

8. Is the child receiving more reinforcement from some other source? (For example, nagging has become reinforcing to a child, or an older brother is egging a younger one on to misbehavior.)

9. Have you been consistent?

10. Have you given the reinforcer a chance to work?

11. What has your behavior been like? If you have been nagging or threatening, you're making it more difficult for yourself. Let the consequences do the work for you.

CHAPTER III

Decreasing Undesirable Behavior

There's no getting around it: some behaviors can't be tolerated. Two-year-olds can't be allowed to run into the street. Fifteen-year-olds can't be allowed to run the house. The whining of a four-year-old becomes exasperating in an eight-year-old, and the temper tantrums of a toddler are tyrannizing in a child of ten. Taking someone else's property is one thing in a kindergarten child, quite another when an older child does it. Besides, whenever a child consistently misbehaves, he is trying to tell you something. You owe it to yourself, and to the child, to listen. Attention, consistency and structure are basic requirements for children; so are limits. Without limits, children will continually push for boundaries to find out where they stand. Misbehavior might mean a child is not receiving enough of these basic ingredients.

The most effective and, in the long run, easiest way to discourage misbehavior is to let children know what you expect and then to reinforce appropriate behavior. The fair-pair technique—building behavior incompatible with what you are trying to discourage—is a method you are already familiar with. This step is imperative in decreasing undesirable behavior. It is not sufficient to teach a child what not to do; he or she must learn what to do in its place.

The basic three-step method discussed in the first two chapters can be used to discourage misbehavior:

1. Identify what behavior is to be discouraged. Use the guidelines in the previous chapter to help you choose this behavior.
2. Intervene. Systematically apply a consequence (when-then) to that behavior.
3. Evaluate. Keep records.

You might find any or all of the following techniques helpful in decreasing undesirable behavior:

1. Changing the situation before misbehavior occurs
2. Letting a child take the consequences of his actions
3. Consciously ignoring the child
4. Removing the child from the situation
5. Punishing the child

Changing the Situation

Sometimes the best way to discourage misbehavior is to make a change in the situation *before* things get out of hand (an ounce of prevention). For example, Maria and Michael Green fought like clockwork every evening before dinner. Their mother dreaded five o'clock, because at that time the teasing would start, and then fighting would follow. Threats and cajoling proved unavailing. Mr. Green didn't get home until a little after six, and by then tempers were short and appetites fierce. After analyzing the situation, Mrs. Green concluded that the children's hunger was making them cranky. She decided to serve them a snack at four-thirty. She also had the children help with the cooking and other preparations for dinner. The children's appetites remained controllable, and they were too busy to get into trouble.

Give children something to do in place of fighting. Buying them bicycles, getting new games and toys, or structuring activities so that children can be involved in them is sometimes all it takes to turn a situation around. The more you encourage constructive activities—be they building block towers, playing Little League ball, or watering plants—the less likely it is that misbehavior will occur. Children who are busy are happy. They become more interested in finishing their project than in teasing and getting into trouble.

Using Natural Consequences

Let the consequences fall on the child, not the parent. A child has to learn to stand on his own two feet one of these days. Why not now, at least as far as he is capable? If you stop bailing your child out, he will learn to bail himself out. More important, he'll stop getting the boat full of water.

My daughter Risa, age fifteen, wore contact lenses. She owned a pair of glasses, but wouldn't wear them because she thought they made her look ugly. Occasionally she would lose her contact lenses. We fumed—and replaced them. Eventually I got tired of it and told Risa she would have to replace them herself if they were lost.

Risa lost them again. My wife and I refused to pay for a new pair. Risa cried and said she'd fail all her school subjects because she couldn't see the board. I suggested she either wear her glasses or babysit to raise the money. She refused. It was a stalemate; Risa proceeded to bite off her nose to spite her face. As her sixteenth birthday approached, Risa asked if she could learn to drive the family car. I told her that with her poor vision it was out of the question. Risa was smart enough to figure out that the school wouldn't let her take driver's education without glasses. She did some babysitting, replaced her contacts, and lost them only once more in the next three years. She had to pay for them then as well.

Another one of our children, Michael, age eight, wasn't very conscientious about putting his soiled clothes in the hamper; he left them near the tub or by his bed. He was used to our picking up after him. We let him know we would no longer do that. If his clothes were not in the hamper, we wouldn't wash them. The clothes piled up. Michael started to wear dirty clothes. We said nothing. After three days, he got the point and began to put his dirty clothes in the hamper. That was seldom a problem again.

Using natural consequences is generally more effective than scolding or punishing. Do not threaten or demand that children do things. Don't back them into a corner. Let them know what will or will not happen and why, and let them make up their own minds. If a child breaks a window playing baseball, he'll have to pay for the window out of his allowance. If the clothes are not in the hamper, they won't get washed. That applies to Daddy, sister, brother and everyone else who is capable of putting things where they belong. If children don't get to the school bus on time, they can walk; or if you have to take them, you will do it at your convenience, not theirs; they'll have to deal with their teacher themselves. If they won't eat the food that is placed on the table, they can make their own, or wait until the next meal is served. If they bring a large group home from school and they're not supposed to, they all have to go home; as long as they've been told beforehand, they have no one to blame but themselves. The idea is to let children know that the world will not cater to them; they must take responsibility for their own actions. Consequences maintain behavior.

A note about selective deafness: most children learn very early in life to distinguish real intentions from idle ones—when a parent means something and when he doesn't. If words are the primary consequences you use with a child, quite often they will fall on deaf ears. Therefore, say something only once, and let the child take the consequences of his actions. You will be surprised at how quickly his hearing will be restored.

Ignoring

Planned ignoring (Don't look now, but . . .) is one of the most effective behavior modification techniques. Behaviors you do not want to see develop—tantrums, whining, argumentativeness, among others—will not develop if they are ignored. Ignoring inappropriate behavior may sound like "head in the sand" advice, but the facts show that behavior decreases in frequency when it is ignored. Constantly telling a child that he does wrong draws a lot of attention to misbehavior, with the likely result that the misbehavior will be reinforced. Consistently ignoring a behavior lets the child know that you will not pay any attention to her for that behavior, and that she will have to behave in other more appropriate ways to get your attention.

Start early with planned ignoring; it will save a lot of energy later on. Take, for example, the "another drink of water" routine which almost every child hits upon. No matter how many times some children get a drink of water, are tucked in and kissed good night, they always want " 'nother drink of water—I'm thirsty."

The Smiths had that problem. They got tough: "No more water; now you go to sleep. . . ." Arguments, crying, whining. They nagged at their son to finish drinking, which only made him drink more slowly. They shouted at him, which gave him a model to copy from. The scenes sometimes went on for thirty or forty minutes, which was just the way their child liked it.

Finally the Smiths decided they had had enough. Mark was given half an apple (non-thirst producing) and a glass of water to put beside his bed. He was told that his parents would no longer answer him if he called out at night. Fifteen minutes later Mark demanded "another drink of water." His parents didn't respond, and his tears flowed like rain. His parents held firm; they knew that if they didn't, Mark would become more and more demanding, and all their suffering during his crying would be wasted. It wasn't easy; Mark had a great pair of lungs. When crying didn't work, Mark informed his parents they were hurting his feelings. They suppressed their giggles and held on. Finally he went to sleep. The second night was better: only ten minutes of uproar. The third night: all quiet. Mark want to sleep peacefully, without asking for that drink of water.

Mark's prolonged tears and intensified attempts to get his parents to come to him could have been expected. There is often a temporary increase in behavior that is ignored. It's like putting a penny in the slot and realizing that no gum is coming out. You shake the machine until you realize it doesn't help. Then you stop.

Mark's behavior proved relatively easy to discourage; not all such problems are so easy to solve. If a child has been crying, whining or throwing tantrums for several years, you cannot change the pattern in one or two days. Often it takes weeks or even months, and you have to carefully reinforce the desired behavior a good deal during that time. It's hard to break old habits—yours as well as a child's—especially when you've been doing something a long time. But if you ever hear yourself say, "How many times have I had to tell you . . . ," you know that your nagging hasn't done much good, so try ignoring instead.

There are many behaviors that can be safely discouraged by ignoring. If a child asks a question in a rude manner, ignore her. Let her know your policy about answering questions. Then answer her quickly and politely when the question is asked in a more acceptable way. Cursing and the use of racial slurs are often attention-getting devices, and if ignored they usually disappear. Ignoring is not always easy to pull off, but it saves a lot of grief later on.

The difficulty with ignoring is that your impulse is to *do* something when a child is misbehaving. Here is where reinforcing yourself can be applied. Instead of telling your daughter for the eighteenth time why she has to be home after school, or hollering at your son when he is whining, lock yourself in the bathroom and take a long, soothing bubble bath. Even little children respect the bathroom as a private place. If your child begins to shout and whine, turn the spigots on full and let the water drown out the noise. The child is more likely to get tired of speaking to a blank wall than you are to get tired of soaking in a hot tub. Eventually your child will get the message: you will not respond to misbehavior.

You must also be sure that what the child is doing isn't more rewarding than your approval or attention. For instance, you could ignore your child's TV viewing, but you probably would not be able to cut it down that way, since TV can be very reinforcing in itself. With that kind of problem, you have to find a more rewarding activity to take the place of the one you're trying to discourage.

Ignoring can also be helpful if a child is going through a phase. David, age four, was gun crazy. His imagination transformed broken twigs into ray guns and branches into machine guns. The noises he made were marvelous to hear. His father, an ardent conservationist, wanted to forbid David to play with guns. David's mother, a nursery-school teacher, felt that that would set up a power struggle which would upset everyone. She suggested to her husband that he wait a month to see what would happen to David's interest in guns. By the end of the month David was into horses and had forgotten about guns.

Another example of ignoring involves a six-year-old who loved to paint. The only color she ever used, however, was black. Her father became concerned about this; he discussed it with his daughter's teacher. The teacher told the father that if Pamela was allowed to use black whenever she wanted, she would probably begin to try new colors in about two weeks. The teacher was right. In two weeks Pamela had tired of using black.

Children, like grownups, will participate in fads and crazes. Left to their own devices, they will eventually change. If they are "forced" to change or if undue attention is paid to their activities, they will dig in their heels and refuse to give up what they are doing. If they do give in because of coercion or manipulation, they will feel resentment toward you.

Children, again like adults, get tired of doing the same things over and over again. They will seek something different if only for novelty's sake. The best course is to let the phase pass. This too might sound like "head in the sand" advice, but the facts are there to back up the statement. Too much of a good thing is still too much! Just think back to the last time you went on a pumpkin-pie–eating orgy, and how long a time elapsed before you repeated it.

When ignoring a child for misbehavior, make sure he or she is not receiving reinforcement from another source for misbehaving—friends or brothers and sisters. Their attention can be more powerful than your ignoring. An effective way of combating this is to reward the potential audience for ignoring misbehavior.

If the behavior is too serious to ignore, there are still other techniques that can be used.

Removing the Child from the Situation

One of the more effective ways of discouraging maladaptive behavior is to remove a child from the situation in which he is misbehaving. This is called time-out, a shorthand expression for time out from positive reinforcement. It is essentially a mild form of punishment. It is most effective when used systematically—that is, every time a child misbehaves in a particular way. Make sure the child doesn't have fun when he is "timed out."

In one family a younger boy often destroyed the block buildings that his older brother laboriously made. His parents handled that problem by placing the child in a time-out area—his bedroom without the TV—every time he did it. They also gave him a reinforcer for *not* doing it. Within three weeks the child had stopped that particular behavior.

Appropriate time-out areas include the bedroom or a chair in the living room or kitchen. Children should *not* be locked in closets or dark rooms. When a child is sent to the time-out area, show him a clock and indicate when he can come out. When he does come out, it is very important to show approval for the things he does right. Timing-out can be a very effective technique, but it can be abused if used too often or for too long a period.

Time-out is particularly effective in helping children learn the difference between indoor and outdoor play. If a child misbehaves in the living room, let him know—once—exactly what he is doing wrong, why it is inappropriate, how it can be corrected, and the consequences that will follow continued misbehavior. This should not be said as a threat or a challenge. The next move is the child's, but now he knows what the limits are. If he continues to misbehave, send him out. Pay no attention to him when he is timed out. If he continues to misbehave, let him know that time-out starts when he quiets down. That is one reason why it's important to be specific about how long the child will have to stay out of the room. Five minutes is usually called for with younger children. Anything less is likely to provide the child with too much attention from the sheer act of getting him out of the room. More time is probably necessary with older children.

If the rest of the family is having fun, the child will get the message: the living room is a fun place to be, but I have to behave to stay there. If a child misbehaves in the kitchen and it's gotten past the point where ignoring will work, send him out and let him wait until the family has finished eating. Then let him eat by himself. Always give the child the opportunity to return to where he was, but let him know that misbehavior will not be tolerated, period.

Time-out can be used quite creatively in a lot of situations. It can even be used to discourage inappropriate speech patterns.

My teenage daughter Amy loved to talk. She picked up the habit of saying "you know" after every sentence. Many people found that irritating. Even her friends didn't enjoy having an extended conversation with her.

My wife and I spoke to her about this pattern. So did her teacher. Amy wanted to control it, but didn't know how. The family decided—with her consent—to time her out for two minutes every time she said "you know." The procedure was based on the assumption that talking was reinforcing to Amy or else she wouldn't do so much of it. When Amy said "you know," her mother or I looked at the clock and said, "Two minutes!" The family members continued their conversation but deliberately excluded her. When the two minutes had passed, Amy was permitted to rejoin the conversation. Within two days the frequency of her saying "you know" had decreased from an average of twenty-three times a day to two times a day. Within a week, "you know" had vanished. The procedure only had to be reinstated twice during the next six-month period.

Punishing

Punishment—that is, imposing unpleasant consequences—can, of course, effectively discourage misbehavior. Every parent punishes a child at one time or another. You have to. Some things—playing with matches, for example—are far too dangerous to ignore. You can't use natural consequences to teach the dangers of traffic. If you find your home a shambles from a teenager's party when you come back from that ski weekend, although you left the children with the understanding there was *not* to be a party, the children need to learn that there are penalties for breaking that sort of agreement. Depriving the children of the car or grounding them (restricting their going out at night or on weekends) can teach that lesson. Always be sure to let the child know what the rules are (if he or she is capable of understanding them) and what the consequences will be for breaking them. Then, if the punishment is administered well, a child will know why he's being punished and won't readily repeat the misbehavior.

Criteria for Using Punishment

Punishment can be an invaluable aid in helping children learn. It can also have far-reaching and negative effects. A balance must be found between the two. The following criteria might be helpful in striking such a balance.

1. Is the punishment justified? Why do you want to inhibit the behavior? Are you trying to impose your will on the child? Is punishment the most effective way to solve the problem? Punishment is only justified if it is likely to inhibit the problem behavior.
2. Is the punishment immediate? Punishment should immediately and inevitably follow specific behavior. It will, of course, be more effective anyway if it is immediate.
3. Is the punishment precise? Punishment, like reward, has to be specific if it is going to work.
4. Is the punishment effective? If the punishment does not in the long run inhibit the behavior, it is not punishment. Try something else if you want results!

Teaching a young child the meaning of "no" is essentially a punishing process. The fewer times you have to do it, the better. When a child is first beginning to walk, it is wise to place fragile objects out of her reach. There will be enough other things that she cannot be allowed to handle, and there's no sense in trying to teach everything at once. But when you do say "no," a child must understand it as a command that *must* be obeyed.

Be consistent with "no"; if a child is allowed to handle the glass ashtray on some occasions but not on others, the message will become confused and she will begin to doubt the validity of your "no." The same kind of consistency will help when you are establishing bedtimes, rules for straightening up, and so forth.

Say "no" in a sharp (but not hysterical) voice. Let a child know that what she is doing is very displeasing to you and why. Teach the words "hot" and "break" along with "no." Try to divert the child to more acceptable things. If a child knows that there are raisins hidden in the pots and pans, those pots and pans will become much more fascinating than the electrical outlet. If the child is not in any immediate danger, say "no" and then exert enough pressure to ease him away from the danger. Reward any withdrawal with your attention. In the beginning, you will probably have to provide alternative objects, but after a while let the child find these things on his own.

Try to say "no" *before* he touches the stove or outlet or other forbidden things. Again, be sure to reinforce his moving away on his own. If he will not heed your command, sharply slap his hands immediately after they touch the dangerous object. First talk, *then* slap. The child will soon learn, if you are consistent, that your warning is real and that unpleasant consequences can be avoided by heeding you. Your hitting will then be quite minimal.

Harsh punishment—physical punishment in particular—is justified in the opinion of most psychologists if it will lead to a rapid reduction of behavior that would only bring a child greater punishment. Running out in the street is an example of behavior that warrants harsh punishment, for failure to learn the lesson might lead to death or serious injury. Biting is another example. If a child is not inhibited from biting—and quickly—he will receive the greater punishment of exclusion from other children. Usually a sharp smack—two or three at the most on the child's buttocks with your open hand is all that is required. A good part of the idea of hitting a child is to let him or her know how serious you consider the offense, and that can be usually conveyed by one smack, particularly if you seldom hit the child. One smack also lets the child know it's going to hurt her if she persists in the misbehavior. She can figure out for herself that you could increase the number of blows if you wanted to. Punishment should be used to help prevent misbehavior, not bring down retribution for it.

Severe punishment is usually not the most effective way to decrease a particular behavior. Most of us tend to use punishment far too readily, and when we inflict too harsh or too frequent punishment on children, we run the risk of arousing anxiety and feelings of revenge and rebellion. Children may follow yet another course and avoid the punisher. These are the classic fight-or-flight reactions. In time, massive anxiety feelings can lead a child to seek out punishment to alleviate the anxiety. Moreover, such punishments as striking a child, locking him in his room, or screaming at him do not always accomplish the hoped-for goals. They probably will have an immediate effect, but if the behavior that led to the punishment does not, in the long run, decrease in frequency and/or intensity, there is a good chance the "punishment" was really a reinforcer and that it encouraged rather than discouraged the negative behavior.

An adolescent girl recently recounted an incident that shows what can happen with the faulty use of punishment. She had broken a lamp. When her mother asked her who did it, the girl refused to answer. The mother said, "God is crying because you're not telling the truth. The Virgin is also crying because she doesn't like girls who lie. Now tell me if you broke the lamp." The moment the girl admitted her guilt, her mother beat her savagely. The girl remarked that neither God nor the Virgin had helped her that day.

"It's no wonder I began to lose my faith then," she said. "I know I learned to lie that day." The deck was stacked against her. The consequence of telling the truth was severe punishment. So it is important not to put children in a position where they are punished for telling the truth.

In addition to being ineffective if too harsh or too frequently used, punishment can instill a basic fear and dislike of the person who does the punishing. If a child perceives a parent as basically punishing and negative, the parent will find it difficult to guide and instruct the child. Besides, one of the greatest dangers in punishment is that children will imitate the punisher, especially if physical force is involved. A child may be unable to strike back at a parent, but he can strike out at a brother or sister or teacher or playmate. Or he may even strike back at himself in one way or another. Violence breeds violence.

Punishing can have a cathartic effect for the adult, but that's not the issue; how to reduce a child's maladaptive behavior is. So if you find yourself relying on punishment a great deal, consider whether your demands are realistic and whether you are going about things in the right way. Something is not right if you have to use this form of discipline often.

Punishment should always be used fairly and matter-of-factly. Hysterical, angry or overemotional responses might make you feel better temporarily, but they provide the wrong model for a child and won't get you far. They teach a child that he can control your emotional state, and he can get quite adept at that with a little practice. Depriving children of privileges is more effective than hitting or screaming. Grounding a child, forbidding the use of TV, and not taking a child on a trip are examples of appropriate punishments.

Make sure the punishment fits the crime and, if possible, is related to it.

David, age five, did not put his bike and toys away after playing outside. His parents had no choice but to move the bike when it blocked the driveway. His father told David that if the bike had to be put away for him, there was no guaranteeing when he would get it back. David forgot. His father stored the bike in such a way that David couldn't get it himself. When he asked for it, he was told that his parents were busy and he'd just have to wait. A few days later they found the time, but not before David missed out on some bike riding. He didn't often leave his bike in the driveway after that.

When you have to put things away for a youngster—things that he should put away himself—do not give them back right away. That will help him learn quickly what he has to do in order to meet his own needs, and other people's too.

Fourteen-year-old Timothy did not do his Saturday chores. He wanted to have his rock band practice at his house. His parents refused to let him have friends over that week. If he didn't help in the house, he could not get the benefits of living in a house.

Always tell a child why he is being punished so that it will be easier for him to learn from the experience. And once the punishment is over, forget about it. If you continually bring up the past, you set negative expectations and fill the child full of doubt as to whether he can do things well.

If you use punishment, keep the following guidelines in mind:

1. Use punishment seldom. Then when you do use it, it will be more effective. Make it very dramatic but not hysterical. Your voice, attitude and demeanor should express a quiet outrage.

2. Use punishment precisely and carefully. The punishment should be given only for a specific behavior, and its effect should be carefully monitored.

3. Be consistent and systematic.

4. After punishing, get reinforcement started quickly for an incompatible behavior. You should make ten encouraging comments for every instance of punishment. The encouraging comments do not have to be related to the problem area, but it helps if they are. Part of this strategy is to help your child see you as an encouraging person, a person he or she wants to please. If you do not see instances where you can be encouraging, your standards are probably too high. You have to start where the child is.

CHAPTER IV

Behavior Modification and Parents

Behavior modification is a two-way street: to make it effective, the parent has to work with himself or herself as well as with the child. If you are tense, distracted or inconsistent, you will be much less likely to get the results you want. Fortunately, there are a number of behavior modification techniques you can use on yourself to promote positive changes in your own behavior.

Reinforcement Systems

Perhaps the easiest way of controlling your own behavior is through a reinforcement system based on the same principles you use with children. First, identify the behavior you want to increase or decrease (use a fair-pair if necessary). Set up an intervention program, and then evaluate the success of your efforts.

Take Carolyn Voss. She was twenty-eight and had a three-year-old son and a five-year-old daughter. The major difficulty she faced as a parent was her feeling of impotence and annoyance when she nagged, and she nagged a lot, because her children didn't put things away. Carolyn's mother had nagged her a great deal, and Carolyn found herself repeating the pattern. She knew she had to change if she was to be more content with herself and more effective as a mother.

Carolyn identified the behavior to be decreased as nagging. As a fair-pair she decided to say something nice to her children and/or file her nails when was tempted to nag. For reinforcement she decided that *when* she had decreased her nagging by half, *then* she would call her friend and catch the matinee she had wanted to see for so long. She bought a wrist counter like those that golfers wear, and every time she nagged, she recorded it.

The first day, she counted nineteen naggings. The next day she got it down to fourteen. Carolyn proudly marked the information down in red on a chart so that everyone could see it. She pasted the chart on the refrigerator and told everyone what she was doing with the wrist counter. She asked everyone to help her by letting her know what a good job she was doing when she wasn't nagging. She also asked them to remind her to record any nagging if they didn't see her record it, as nagging might occur without her being aware of it. Her idea was sensible. Most of us need all the help and support we can get in overcoming bad habits, and when you've been doing something for a long time, you're not always aware that you're doing it. More eyes, or in this case ears, help you become more aware of yourself.

By the end of the week she was down to eight naggings, and she rewarded herself by going to the play. She followed a similar system for the next two weeks, rewarding herself with a visit to a friend and dinner out. She also continued the system after that to prevent the habit from reappearing. Carolyn soon succeeded in getting the nagging down to one or two a day, a frequency that she felt she and her children could live with.

Carolyn also handled the problem of the children's untidiness by motivating them to clean up. When it worked she felt good about that too. Becoming more effective as a parent is another way to give yourself pleasure. The wonderful thing about it is that everybody benefits.

When you are distressed by a pattern you seem to be following, count your own behavior. Just as Carolyn reduced her nagging by observing it, you can count—and then reduce—your own threats, yelling, hitting, self-pitying statements and any other behavior that is obnoxious to you and that you would like to curtail. More important, perhaps, you can stimulate more positive interaction by reinforcing yourself for encouraging, praising, and showing appreciation for appropriate behavior, whether the behavior is yours or the youngster's.

You can also help solve problems more efficiently and more peacefully that way. Usually, what you do is the key to a problem with a child. This does not mean you caused the problem. It does mean you can help solve the problem and change the way you feel about it.

Behavior modification can also help you to be more positive with your spouse. This in turn can lead to more positive interactions with the children.

Martha Greer had a self-defeating habit. Whenever she left the children with her husband, she would come home to find the house a mess. She invariably started hollering and telling her husband what a terrible housekeeper he was, and how he obviously didn't take care of the children very well if that was how they left the house. He became more and more reluctant to stay at home with the children and began finding other things to do. His avoidance increased her resentment.

During one of their arguments he told her he felt punished by her every time he stayed home to watch the kids. She thought about it a while and realized his words made sense. Martha then began to reinforce his help with the children, and he did more of it. She also asked him if he would be sure to pick things up. She was explicit about what was important to her. Martha consciously remarked on the good things he did, and he felt more appreciated. He ended up spending more time with the children and straightening up after himself, and they were both happier.

Relaxation

Relaxation is another behavior modification technique you can use to make yourself feel better. Relaxation is one of the most effective means we know of to reduce tension. It is based on the premise that anxiety (general tension and a sense of fear and uncertainty) cannot coexist with a state of physical relaxation. Anxiety and tension cause muscles to tighten. This in turn causes the stomach to tense and your breathing to become irregular. Too much anxiety and stress can manifest themselves in such symptoms as stomach upset, diarrhea, insomnia, and temper tantrums. But even a little tension can cause general irritability.

Tension lodges throughout the body and affects all the muscles. Tense muscles use up a lot of energy—something parents never have enough of. Relaxation—the actual physical release of tension in muscles—can help a person through stress. It will not take away the problems that caused the anxiety or stress, but it can help you cope with them better because your body and mind aren't using up a lot of the energy that you need to deal with the problem itself. Moreover, when your body is relaxed, your mind is more efficient and capable, and you can keep problems in perspective.

Specifically, you can use relaxation to help take your daughter's whining in stride, especially when you know everything will be okay if you can just ignore it a little longer. It can also help you put up with the thought of having to cook another meal at the end of a busy day, or the anticipation of the storm Johnny will raise when he discovers he doesn't have enough points for the camping trip he wanted to take (but not so badly that he was willing to do his chores for it). Relaxing yourself can also help you to bide your time while waiting for your child to finish his or her homework or temper tantrums, or to summon enough strength to call your children downstairs to put away their plates. Some people use relaxation instead of a martini to help them unwind at the end of the day, or to prepare themselves for sleep.

In essence, the idea of relaxation is to get the muscles to rid themselves of tautness and to put your body and mind at ease. This is done by deliberately tightening the muscles, one group at a time, and then slowly releasing the tension you created. You should not do this if you are suffering from whiplash or other strains. Otherwise, no matter how strong or weak you are, you should have little trouble with the procedure.

It's best to go through the sequence with your eyes shut. Here's how to do it:

> Sit by yourself in a comfortable chair. Do not cross your legs. Keep your mouth open a little. Distractions such as radios, kids' hollering, or the demands of others should be guarded against. You have to concentrate to relax. Your arms should be by your sides with the fingers open. If stray thoughts enter your mind, shoo them away by saying STOP to yourself and bringing yourself back to the job at hand.
>
> Start with your arms. Make a fist with the right hand and flex your right biceps by drawing your arm up toward your body as if you were a muscle man at the beach. Hold the muscle taut for ten seconds or until it feels strained. Then relax it by letting go of the tension slowly. "Slowly" means it should take about five seconds for your arm to descend from the taut position to your lap. Wait about

twenty seconds and then flex the other arm. Follow the sequence of ten seconds taut, five seconds to relax the muscle, and a twenty-second pause.

Now lift your right leg up so that it extends straight out (it's not essential that you have your shoes off, but it's more comfortable). Point your toes downward until you feel tension in the arch of your foot and in the thigh muscle itself. Hold your leg taut for ten seconds—not so tight that it is strained, but tight enough to feel the tension. Now relax the muscle and slowly let your leg down. Concentrate on relaxing all the muscles in your leg that are taut, pausing for twenty seconds each time your leg is down. Then do the left leg in the same way.

Now squeeze your buttocks together. Hold it that way for ten seconds and then very slowly relax the tension. When the tension is free from that area, concentrate on your stomach. Tighten up the muscles there as if someone were going to throw a medicine ball into your stomach. Get the muscles good and tight. Hold the tension for ten seconds and then relax slowly. Try to relax the muscles deep inside your belly. When those muscles are relaxed, just breathe slowly and deeply, in and out.

Then arch your back, especially the small of the back. When you feel the tension build up, hold it for ten seconds. Concentrate on your breathing and let go of the tension. Now return to your regular sitting position. Let your back feel limp, as if you had just taken a great strain off it and are resting. Again concentrate on taking long, slow breaths.

Next comes the chest. Take a deep breath and hold it. As you hold your breath, the tension in your chest will build up. Hold your breath for fifteen seconds. Then, as slowly as you can, let the air out. Then resume breathing in and out, slowly and deeply, as if you were in a sound sleep.

Now work on the muscles between the shoulder blades and the muscles of the neck. For many people this is an area where muscles actually ache. Pull your shoulders back as far as you can without straining yourself. Try to get your shoulder blades as close as you can to each other, and at the same time arch your neck so that your chin is pointing to the ceiling. Hold the muscles so taut that it is almost a strain. Hold the tightness for ten seconds, then very slowly relax the muscles and move back to your previous position. Let all the tension flow out so that you feel very calm, very relaxed—as if your head were not really supported, but just falling limply against a big stuffed pillow. Pause another twenty seconds, and then move on to the muscles around the face.

First, arch your eyebrows as high up as they can go. Hold those muscles taut for ten seconds. Then slowly let them relax. Squeeze your eyes shut as tightly as you can. Slowly, slowly relax those muscles. Your eyelids will feel heavy, but do not fall asleep; just concentrate on relaxing. Bite hard with your back teeth and press them together until you feel tension in your jaw. Hold it for ten seconds and then let go slowly. You should also feel tension around your temples, and this too will relax as you unclamp your teeth.

Next push your tongue against the roof of your mouth. Relax and let go, slowly. Your teeth should be slightly parted and your jaw hanging slack. Now just concentrate on your breathing—let the breath go in and out of your body slowly and rhythmically.

Now on to the muscles around the mouth and chin. The best way to relax these muscles is to make the widest grin you can. Try to look like Bozo the Clown. Show all your teeth. Let the tension build up for ten seconds. When all the muscles in that group are good and tight, slowly let them go. Expel some air from your nose and throat. Let the tension go out of your throat, the place where you swallow and where your voice box is. Breathe deeply and calmly.

Ask yourself if there is any tension left in your body. If there is, let it out. Let your arms get limp and heavy, as well as your neck muscles and thighs and buttocks. Just let it all flow out and keep on concentrating on your breathing.

Now, with your eyes closed, picture yourself in the middle of a pleasant scene. Make it a peaceful, restful scene, like lying on the beach all alone, where even reading a book seems too much trouble. Imagine the sound of the water and of the gulls, the patch of beach tar on your heels, and the feel of salt in the air. If the scene you have imagined is a meadow, capture the rustle of the leaves in the wind and the smell of thyme slowly filling your nostrils. Imagine yourself relaxing all alone in that pleasant setting, and concentrate on your breathing.

Stay that way for a few minutes. If your mind wanders, bring it back again. If you want to think, think about what a wonderful person you are, what a good mother (father) you are, how pretty or handsome you are. Imagine people complimenting you. You should tell yourself these things all the time, but they take hold better when you are relaxed.

When psychologists use this technique with clients, they often ask the people to put a subjective numerical value on their state of relaxation. Zero would be the calmest one could possibly be, and one hundred would be the most uptight and tense. The psychologist and client strive to get the tension down to between zero and ten on this subjective scale. A person's anxiety level can be lowered considerably by concentrating on breathing, by relaxing tense muscle groups, or just by dwelling on the pleasant scene he or she has created. If you use this exercise, you should keep at it until your state of relaxation is down to practically zero.

After you have practiced these exercises for a while, you will be able to reach a relaxed state in a very short period of time, a few minutes at the most. You can then use this technique to get you through some rough spots. You can also use it in conjunction with another behavioral technique, desensitization.

Desensitization

In desensitization, you imagine what you fear or are uncomfortable with while in a relaxed state. The anxiety attached to what you're uncomfortable about diminishes when it is paired with relaxation. You can then gradually acclimate yourself to the thing you fear. In behavior therapy the psychologist relaxes the client and then, either in imagination or using the real object of fear, gets the client to overcome the anxiety. For example, if a client is afraid of flying, the therapist might relax the person and have him imagine he is twenty miles away from the airport. When the person reports that his anxiety scale is down to near zero, the psychologist has him imagine he is within ten miles of the airport, and so on until the person can actually imagine he is in a plane and is calm. Dealing with very serious matters requires a good deal of technical skill; I am not suggesting that you use this technique on yourself for every anxiety you may suffer from. However, it can be used quite effectively on many common parental problems. Let's take two examples.

Esperanza Montez had two children, eight and six, who in her opinion were wonderful. She often wished, however, that they would finish their chores before they left for school. She decided she could change things if she served breakfast *after* the children had met their responsibilities. She tried that once or twice, but it didn't work out, because she couldn't follow through. She knew she wasn't helping herself or her children that way, but the thought of letting her children go hungry was hard to take.

Mrs. Montez then tried imagining her children going without food for the morning. First she thought about them during recess and on the playground. In her mind they did not appear to be suffering too much. She imagined them just before lunch, ravenously watching the second hand ticking away. In her imagination she saw them as hungry, but not exactly emaciated. In fact, they looked quite robust. This image gave her the resolve to stick to her guns.

The next day she announced her new policy and why she was putting it into effect. Predictably, the children didn't do their chores. True to her word, Mrs. Montez let them go to school without their meal. There were few times after that when she had to remind them to do their chores.

Peter, an adolescent, decided he wanted to grow a beard. His parents recoiled. Luckily they realized their son was past the stage where his parents could tell him whether or not to shave. They knew they would have to accept their child as he was if they were to avoid crises and scenes.

The parents tried desensitization. They relaxed and imagined their son wearing a Brooks Brothers suit and a beard. When they could tolerate that, they imagined him in a sports jacket, shirt and tie with a briefcase and a beard. Gradually they changed the images, cutting out first the briefcase, then the tie, and so on until they could picture their bearded son in tattered jeans, a sweatshirt and sandals. Once they could abide that image, they were able to tolerate the downy fuzz on his cheeks and accept their child as he was.

You can also use this technique in other ways. If you have been avoiding a confrontation with your child about something, go through it in your imagination. You are quite likely to find that it is not as bad as you had first thought, especially if you relax yourself first.

Keeping a Diary

Two other methods can help you. The first is keeping a diary. It combats the feeling, "I haven't done anything today and my life is slipping away." Simply writing down all the things you actually do accomplish in one day can be pleasantly shocking. Parenting is an enormous job, one that requires scores of decisions and hours of work each day. It is too easy to forget that. Keeping a record can help you, and others if necessary, to appreciate what you actually do.

Mrs. Jones was depressed. She felt that she didn't do anything all day. As part of a therapy program, she kept a diary. She put down everything she did: helping the children get off to school in the morning, cleaning the house, preparing supper, paying the bills—all the nitty-gritty details of how she spent her day. When she took a look at what she did, she quickly got over the feeling that she wasn't accomplishing anything. She was also able to understand her depression and lack of energy a little better. Working out a better schedule and dividing up the responsibilities in a fairer way turned out to be more beneficial than six therapy sessions for her.

Thought Stopping

Thought stopping can also be used to help parents. In thought stopping you go through a typically futile thought sequence in your imagination. For example, "I'll never get this house cleaned in time for the company," or "I'll never be able to change my child's behavior; Johnny will always misbehave." Thoughts about how neglected your children are because you went to a movie would also belong in this category.

Every time you get one of those self-defeating and futile thoughts, say STOP to yourself, subvocally. The thoughts will no doubt return, but every time they do, interrupt them again and switch onto a favorite fantasy or something more pleasant. Then go on with your work. The idea is to cut off those futile thoughts at birth, and you can do this by concentrating on something else. This technique does not work with everyone, but it's worth a two-week trial.

Let's look at how some other behavior modification methods can be applied to problems many parents face.

The Inability to Say "No"

Lots of parents get themselves into trouble because they can't say "no." Their children get into a lot of trouble too. This failure doesn't apply only to crisis situations. Failing to say "no" can start when a three-year-old wants you to play on the floor with him and you agree, even though you want to play on the table. It can manifest itself in many little ways, but the upshot is that if you cannot say "no," you yield with reluctance. Reluctance turns into resentment quite easily, and resentment usually turns into anger. It is easier on everyone in the long run if you say "no" when you mean no and "yes" when you mean yes.

One way you can help yourself here is to list all the areas you have trouble with. A sample list might include some of these problems: playing with a child when you don't want to; letting children come home later than the time you agreed upon; letting a teenager take your clothing; letting your children yell at you; not saying anything when children bring friends home for supper without telling you.

It's not always easy to say "no" when you want to and should. But you have to, or your children will take advantage of you. Practice saying "no" in your imagination. Go over one or two scenes when you wanted to put your foot down but didn't, and say to yourself what you should have done. Try out, in your imagination, different and more constructive ways of saying what you want to say. Then try one out in real life. It won't be perfect the first time you say it, but it will be an improvement over wishing you had said it.

If you're having particular trouble with something, ask your partner or a friend for help. Analyze the situation with him or her. Role-play it. First you play the child and let your partner play you. Learn from the way he or she behaves, and then switch roles. Get some constructive feedback. Have the other person model the way it can be done. Keep on practicing until you can say "no" in a convincing way. With young children, the fewer words you use, the better. If Mary squirts her water pistol around the house, just take it away from her without any big to-do. You want to concentrate more on decisiveness—your look and walk and actions—than on verbalization.

When you do have to use words, be aware that how you say "no" is often as important as the word itself. You are the parent, and there will be many times when you will have to say "no." When you have to lay down the law, it is most effective if done in a calm, firm and authoritative voice. Expect that children will respect your rights, just as you respect theirs, and you will get the respect you deserve. The problem of "respect" is a sore subject with many parents. When you feel it is lacking in your children, it sometimes helps to give a thought to whether all your behavior inspires respect. You might also want to ask your children what specific behaviors you need to practice, or not practice, to merit their respect.

Idle Threats

Keep a record of the number of idle threats you make and the number of times you follow through on what you say you will do. Write down what you threatened and then whether you carried it out or not. Sometimes—usually, in fact—threats are made in anger and are much too harsh. Looking at what you said you'd do an hour after you said it can prevent you from overstating your case the next time.

Concentrate on using positive consequences to motivate your child to do better. When a child does not earn them, recognize that it is his or her decision and not yours. Set up a self-reinforcement system for cutting down on your threats and/or following through on them.

Failing to Follow Through on Promises

Publicly posting in red what you said you would do and when you would do it makes it harder for you to fail to follow through on promises. In addition, set a penalty for yourself if you don't follow through. Doing the children's chores for a week might be just the incentive you need. In extreme cases write out a check to your most hated political cause and let the child mail it if you fail to follow through. The reminders to send them more money and the notes you'll get throughout the year expressing their appreciation for your support will motivate you in a positive direction. Also reward yourself when you meet a specific goal that was decided on beforehand.

Blowups

For blowups, try a reinforcement program similar to the one Carolyn Voss used for nagging. Keep a record and reward yourself for a reduction in blowups. Attach a penalty to blowups if necessary. Have your children count the blowups and record them. Do their chores for them or take them out to dinner if you exceed the quota.

Also try relaxation and desensitization to whatever is causing you to blow up. It might not be the fact that Johnny leaves his socks on the bathroom floor that causes your extreme emotion as much as your fear that you are losing authority. You'll have to decide that. When you analyze the problem, you may also find that you are not saying "no" when you should. Consequently, it is possible you are blowing up over the wrong issues.

In addition to working on yourself, set up an explicit program to change the children's behavior if they are doing something they shouldn't be doing.

Feeling Guilty and Inadequate as a Parent

To combat guilt feelings, rationally examine whether you are meeting the basic health and safety requirements of your children and providing them with the love and care they need.

If your feelings have a rational base you'll have to work on whatever the real problem is. Remember that you don't have to do all the work yourself. If you're too tired to play with your three-year-old in the afternoon, you can invite a friend over for him or her. You just have to see that a child's needs are met, not meet them all yourself.

If your feelings do not have a rational base, take a hard look at what you do. Keep the diary mentioned before. Figure out what it is possible to do in a day, and what you'll be satisfied with. There is no substitute for having explicit day-to-day goals. Recognize that growth comes in small stages.

Thought stopping can also help. So can desensitizing yourself to whatever you feel guilty or inadequate about. Some parents find it helpful to relax themselves and then make up statements in their imaginations about what good parents they are. You can also reenact in your mind all the good things you have done in this area.

Finally, it helps to realize there is no such thing as a perfect parent. Everyone wants to do more for his or her child, but people can only do what they can do. A little self-acceptance goes a long way.

CHAPTER V

Eating

Meal time should be an occasion to relax a little, satisfy hunger, and enjoy good company and good food. Sometimes, though, so much emotional energy gets invested in worries that food and meals become an area of strife and tension.

Among typical problems parents face with eating are a child who finds it difficult to adjust to routines, a child who eats too little or too much, and a child who will only eat certain foods. Parents of children of all ages face these problems. Lucky parents only have difficulties during certain periods of their child's growth; others face them throughout their child's development. But it doesn't have to be that way.

It helps to recognize from the start that some children approach feeding eagerly and love new foods, just as they take to most new experiences easily. Others take a lot longer to warm up to things and approach life more gingerly. Wise parents recognize and accept a child's temperament. Every child brings his or her own vitality, appetite and disposition to eating.

Many children also grow up to be pretty much like their parents as far as food is concerned. Most of children's likes and dislikes develop in response to what is served to them, and to the kinds of messages their parents (and friends) give them about food. Boys and girls also usually end up with manners that are very similar to those of their parents.

In the long run, imitation, for better or worse, is an important determinant of what a child does. A child is more likely to do as he sees than as he's told. So if you can accept yourself, you can probably accept most of your child's manners and mannerisms.

Children's tastes change as they grow up. A child may develop intense likes and dislikes for particular foods and carry these likes and dislikes to extremes. It all tends to balance out, however, in time.

Parents can help their children find this balance by offering a wide variety of food from all the basic food groups.* It is also a good idea not to attach too much importance to any *particular* food. Concentrate instead on providing all the necessary nutrients and vitamins from each group—e.g., protein can come from nuts as well as meat, and calcium from cheese as well as milk. If a parent tries to force a child to eat oatmeal, the child's energies will be invested in proving he doesn't have to eat oatmeal no matter what anyone says. His distaste for oatmeal will linger long after the argument has been forgotten. The fewer power struggles and negative associations there are with food, the greater the likelihood that a child will like at least some foods from every basic group needed for growth. Where possible, give children choices about what to eat.

Now let's begin at the beginning.

Breast Feeding

Three elements are needed for an adequate milk supply. The first is an adequate diet on the part of the mother, which will be assumed here. The second is adequate stimulation of the mammary glands. This can be achieved by letting the infant suck on the breasts, even if no milk comes out. Sucking will bring the milk out after a while. Some women give up too easily when all it might take is a little more time. The third is a relaxed mother. Even if the milk is flowing adequately, too much tension can cause it to stop.

Avoid tension whenever possible during this period. You have a right to be catered to. When it is not possible to avoid tension, deep muscle relaxation and other behavioral techniques might be helpful.

---

* The U.S. Department of Agriculture puts out a host of publications on this subject. They are objective, to the point, and inexpensive. The pamphlet *Nutrition* (1971) will tell you just about everything you need to know about the basic food groups.

Teething can present another complication to a nursing mother. Some babies like to bite the nipple during breast feeding. He or she might think it's a great game, and besides, it relieves the pressure on the gums. Obviously a mother can't allow this. You can't use reasoning very effectively with an infant, so you'll have to teach him or her the consequences of biting. If and when the infant bites the nipple, say "no" in a sharp manner and withdraw the breast. Put your finger in his or her mouth and voice disapproval. (At first the infant won't know the significance of the finger, but it will become a warning to him or her.) Then go back to nursing. If it happens a second time, say "no" in the same sharp voice and withdraw the breast. This time do not let the infant suck at it again. The infant will learn that biting equals the withdrawal of the breast. If the infant is still hungry, he or she can always eat later on. Most biting occurs, however, at the end of a feeding, so hunger usually won't be a problem. At the beginning of the feeding most babies are so hungry they're content just to suck. After a while they catch on to the fact that they can get more pleasure from sucking than from biting.

Schedules

Babies can be placed on self-demand schedules, where they are fed whenever and for as long as they want, or they can be taught to follow a regular feeding pattern. A schedule is always set up to help the baby, but a reasonable schedule helps the parents too.

Most babies start off eating six or seven times a day. The goal is to increase the amount of time between feedings. This will automatically decrease the number of meals. If you want to set up a schedule, plan to feed the infant at regular intervals. Begin moving her onto a regular schedule by very gradually increasing the amount of time between feedings.

If the baby wakes up before the time for her feeding, leave her alone; she may go back to sleep. You do not want her to get into the habit of having small feedings at short intervals. If the baby wakes up for good, then cuddle or rock her, or play a game like Peek-a-Boo. You then reinforce the waiting while you're both enjoying yourselves. The reinforcement might be just as satisfying as food. If the baby begins to cry in earnest, try a pacifier or a bottle of water instead of food. That will usually keep her contented and help her to adjust to a longer interval between feedings.

If she insists on being fed, feed her. At that age her stomach pains take precedence over your convenience.

Babies usually give up the early morning (two o'clock) feeding first. Help this along by delaying the night feeding for as long as you can. Play with the baby at night and divert her from her feeding for as long as she's willing. The later she eats and the more she eats at that feeding the better, for the longer she'll sleep. She'll gradually begin to get up later and later for the night bottle until one night she'll sleep right through.

Chronologically, most babies are ready for a three-meal-a-day schedule at between four and six months, but you of course have to guide yourself by how long your baby can go between meals without showing discomfort. Supplementary bottles or snacks can be used to get a child through the adjustment period.

If the baby eats well only at every other meal, place her on a three-meal-a-day schedule right away. Her poor appetite is probably a simple case of not being very hungry. When a child eats reluctantly, dawdling, throwing food, and power struggles often develop later.

The trick to evolving a schedule is to do it gradually. Let hunger, not your coaxing, provide motivation for a feeding. If necessary, divert the baby before the feeding so that a longer and longer time elapses between meals. Don't interpret every cry as a call for food. Don't give a baby the idea that all her needs can be met through eating. Nature will push her onto a schedule. All you have to do is help a little.

Some parents feel guilty about putting an infant on a schedule. There is no need to. It can only help the child in the long run, and parents' needs must be considered too. In scheduling, guide yourself by what is fair to the child *and* convenient for you. The fact that a child is willing to eat every three or four hours should not be the primary consideration. The question is whether the child can go for longer periods of time without discomfort, and what the needs of the whole family are.

If the baby is gaining weight but often wakes up crying, hunger is probably not the reason for the discomfort. Some possibilities are insufficient sucking, indigestion, temperament or colic (the latter should be diagnosed by a physician). Try giving the baby his thumb or a pacifier if he cries. It's good for a baby to suck, despite some myths to the contrary. Burping is still the best cure for indigestion. Massage has been found to be helpful for fretfulness and colic, although the relief it affords the baby is usually only temporary. Console yourself with the fact that weight gain is a more reliable indicator of a baby's well-being than tears.

There's no doubt that crying jags are hard on a parent. Deep muscle relaxation and desensitization might help you to cope. You can also take a shower. The sound of the water will drown out the noise, at least for a while. It might also help to realize that babies outgrow this period of discomfort.

Solid Foods

Cereal is usually the first solid a baby eats, but it makes more sense to give fruit to fretful infants. Most children take to fruit very easily. Which you use first is not important; whether the infant likes it and wants more is. Serve a variety of fruits and cereals so that the baby can get used to different foods from the beginning of his or her life. Be patient, because a baby has to learn to like things. At the beginning a teaspoon or less should be given. Actually, a demitasse spoon is a lot more comfortable for infants.

Motivation always makes teaching easier. Therefore, introduce solid foods to a baby when he or she is hungriest. Hunger will motivate the baby to find out what that substance in his mouth is. Whatever meal a child eats most readily is the meal to start with. This rules applies to the introduction of any new food at any age. The hungrier a child is, the more readily he or she will take to a new food—or at least give it a try.

There is no payoff in trying to force a child to eat any particular food. Reinforcement works much better. At the same time, do not yield too easily to a child's tastes. Many times parents are so happy to see their child eat that they let him make all the decisions regarding food. If you do that, there is always the danger that the child will insist on the tried and true. When introducing a new food, give him a tiny spoonful of it. Hold it in his mouth for a while if necessary. Then follow it up with a spoonful of food that he likes. Keep on alternating spoonfuls. If a food that the child likes is given immediately after he eats the new food, the process of acquiring a taste for the strange food will move along more rapidly. And, by all means, don't forget the value of reinforcement—verbal and nonverbal—when the child accepts a new food in his diet. If a youngster has given a new food a fair try and still doesn't like it, don't force the issue. Switch to something else. Meals should never be a battleground, because there are no winners in food struggles.

Weaning

The earlier you start to wean a child, the easier it is, for at twenty to twenty-four weeks the child is not fixed in his or her habits. However, there is nothing wrong with weaning at a later age.

The goal in weaning, of course, is to help a child learn to drink from a cup or glass. You need to reinforce all the steps that lead to that goal. You first want the infant to get used to the idea that liquids can come from cups as well as from nipples. Start by giving the baby a sip of milk or some other liquid from a cup. Express delight when he or she takes a drink that way. Model the behavior as well. Put some water or juice in a cup and drink from it. Let the baby know how delicious it is by smacking your lips and showing great enthusiasm. Then give the baby his or her turn. Keep on taking turns, each person taking a sip or two. At first you should hold the cup, because most babies can't manage it by themselves until they are approximately six months old.

Getting the youngster his or her own cup is also helpful. Let the baby play with the cup. The more a child plays with cups and glasses, the more readily he or she will learn to grasp them firmly. Reinforce this behavior by giving the baby a snack—a raisin or cereal bit—when he holds the cup correctly. Placing the snack in the cup will also help the baby to form pleasant associations with cups.

Often babies will pretend to drink from the cup. Encourage this by pretending you're drinking from the cup too. Place a few drops of milk or juice in the cup during this game once in a while.

When you begin to wean in earnest, give the baby some milk from the cup at each meal. Take advantage of the baby's hunger by offering the cup at the beginning of the meal. You don't want the baby to think about the breast or bottle then, so keep the nipple out of sight.

When the baby becomes accustomed to drinking from the cup, give her a whole meal's supply that way. When she does well on breakfast, start on lunch. Try to make as few changes as possible during that period. For instance, it would not be a good idea to change the child's room or begin toilet training during the weaning period.

Once you decide to wean the baby, it is best to be consistent. That might also mean being firm. If the baby fusses for a while, ignore it. If mother's or father's will collapses under the baby's crying and the child is given the nipple, it is very likely the child will learn there is a real payoff to crying. The rule is that once you have adopted a course of action, stick with it.

One further note should be added here. When you wean, try to do it completely. Many parents allow a child to take the bottle to bed. This probably facilitates falling asleep, but it also creates a dependency on the bottle which is more and more difficult to break as the child gets older. So think about which problem you want to have. Most parents report that it is easier to break the bottle habit completely than to do it in stages.

If the baby wants to suck at night, help him find his thumb for that purpose. Some dentists might object, but sucking is an important element of your child's psychological growth. Unless an issue is made of the thumb-sucking at night, he will probably soon outgrow it.

Keep in mind that it really doesn't matter whether a child is weaned at eight months or twelve months or twenty months. If it's not a problem to you, it won't be a problem to your youngster. Try not to make comparisons between your child and your neighbor's, and don't harangue the baby. If you feel that your baby is too old for a bottle and/or is being subjected to too much pressure and ridicule from sources over which you have no control, wean the child. If you encounter undue difficulty, try the following reinforcement method.

Put some flavoring in the cup, preferably the kind that will both sweeten and change the color of the milk. As the baby begins to drink more and more from the cup, decrease—very gradually, of course—the amount of flavoring you use. Cereals can be used the same way as flavoring. Make the cereal thinner and thinner over time, and do not give the youngster a spoon. Berries can also be used to great advantage. Let the child watch you put her favorite berries into the bottom of the cup. Make eating the berries dependent on emptying the cup (in her mouth, of course). At first use very little milk. Then, when she gets used to the idea of drinking her milk from the cup and getting the berries as a reward, add more milk to the cup very gradually. Give her lots of smiles and hugs when she drinks from the cup and none when she drinks from the bottle.

Some other techniques are the following. Be slow in giving the child a bottle so she will learn that hunger can be satisfied more quickly by drinking from a cup. Hunger is a great motivator for weaning. Do not be too quick to give in if a baby balks at a cup. If nothing else works, you can skip a feeding or decrease the amount of solid food the baby receives. This is usually sufficient motivation to get the baby started on at least one cup of milk a day. Or you can always wean more gradually by letting the child know that she has to take a little bit of milk from the cup before she gets the bottle or the breast. All you have to do then is gradually increase the amount of milk she is required to drink from the cup before she can use a nipple. Keep on giving the child juice and water from the cup to get her used to it.

You can also give the baby a bottle with a very small hole in the nipple so that she has to work very hard to get any milk. A variant of this technique is to gradually make the nipple hole larger and larger so that the child ends up drinking instead of sucking. As you meet success, eliminate first one bottle and then another.

Self-feeding

Independence in eating does not evolve automatically; it has to be prepared for. As soon as a child can pick up things, put some pieces of apple, zweiback, boned chicken or other hand-held edibles on his highchair tray.

Letting the child feed himself that way sets the stage for independence in eating and develops dexterity and coordination. Gradually decrease the size of pieces as the child develops more dexterity. Parents who are quick to note and nurture these tiny evidences of growth give their child a valuable sense of his own possibilities.

When you serve pureed foods, keep an extra spoon or two on the eating surface. Babies love to fool with utensils. The more you let them, the more practice they get in grasping and holding, and the more likely they are to attempt to feed themselves. At twelve months a baby loves to try to use the spoon to feed himself. If he has been encouraged, he can usually do a pretty good job at fifteen months. Encourage him by guiding his hands a little when he tries to get the spoon from the bowl to his mouth. Let go just before he puts the spoon in his mouth. Praise him lavishly for this growth. Gradually begin to guide less and less. Then slow down your feeding more and more. In the beginning you will probably give a child ninety-five percent of the food he takes during his meals. Begin to decrease this percentage to the point where you put in a spoonful and he or she does the same. Use judgment, but when a child slows down, slow down as well, so he will have a reason to continue feeding himself. When babies do not use utensils to feed themselves, it is usually because they have no reason for doing so. You do not have to worry that a baby will starve; he won't.

Food Struggles

Feeding problems often develop at an early age. Between six months and a year a youngster's appetite begins to flag, and his body begins to catch up to the size of his head. Urging a baby to eat more than she needs or wants is a primary reason for feeding problems. The guiding philosophy behind this push seems to be that if some food is good, more food is better. Some babies do eat more and more at their parents' urging, and thus set a pattern for being overweight. But the majority of babies who are urged to eat more than they want simply balk. Then the struggle begins in earnest. Far better to let the baby's natural appetite set the pace. Unless there is an insufficient weight gain or unless a vital element is missing from a child's diet, it is best to let her eat what she wants, and as little or as much as she wants. It all tends to balance out in the long run.

Parental overattention is not the only cause of food struggles. Babies sometimes balk at eating because of irritability or illness or even too much attention (as the child sees it) paid to a brother or a sister. The birth of a new baby is a classic reason for children to start food struggles. Whatever the reason, some children will notice if a parent overreacts to the question of food and exploit it. Being able to control a parent's emotional state is a pretty powerful weapon to place in the hands of a young child, and most of them will, of course, misuse it. That is where your knowledge of behavior principles comes in.

Some specific steps that you can take follow. Communicate to your child, nonverbally if necessary, that you expect him to eat and will provide him with all the good food he wants. At the same time, make it clear that the choice of eating or not eating is entirely his, and that you will not make him eat or even pay any attention to him if he does not eat. You can do this with school-age children as well as with young children. Do not let them snack, and serve food only at mealtimes. Give the reluctant eater very small portions, and serve only the foods that he currently likes best. At this point, don't worry too much about getting a child to eat a balanced diet. That can come later.

Note carefully when your child eats most. Keep records if necessary. Jot down how much he eats in how long when you're there, and compare the results with data on times you're not there. If you find that the child eats better when you are with him, keep him company during the meal. Use your attention selectively. Talk and play with him while he's eating. Break off the play and even eye contact with him when he dawdles. If you find it difficult to ignore the dawdling, leave him alone during the meal and let him make the decision by himself as to whether he wants to eat or not. If you have a hard time staying out of the picture, clean out a cabinet or wash down a wall. Do *anything* that will keep you busy and out of the struggle.

When the child eats a little, give him a tiny bit more; follow his lead. Increase the portions minutely. If the child wants to dawdle and play with his meal, let him. But at the end of thirty minutes take the plate away and let him know that that meal is over. Tell him he can eat again during the next meal. Be matter of fact about it and don't—ever—threaten, scold, cajole, or let him nibble between meals. Hunger will soon motivate him to eat, particularly if he finds he can't get a rise out of you by not eating. This technique can be used with older children as well as young ones.

Most reluctant eaters get upset when they see that their parents are no longer making a fuss about their not eating. Young children will sometimes throw food to provoke a reaction from you. Simply remove the food when that happens. The child will be more reluctant to throw food around the next time. It is a rare child who will not move into a regular feeding pattern after a day or so of this routine, particularly if you reinforce what he does right.

What if a child doesn't begin voluntarily to eat foods that are essential to his health and well-being? In that case, more direct guidance is needed, and Grandma's Law can help set things right.

When my youngest son David was five, he disliked meat and vegetables with a passion. We couldn't find any substitutes for these foods, so we were very concerned. Then I remembered Grandma's Law: you may have your ice cream when you've finished your spinach. It happened that David was a pushover for french fried potatoes, so I decided to try behavior modification, using the french fries as a reinforcer.

I cooked up a batch of crisp, sizzling french fries and placed them where David could see and smell—but not touch—them. I invited David to eat five bite-size pieces of roast beef and two forkfuls of buttered carrots, for which he would receive an entire plateful of french fries. The temptation was too much for David. He downed the meat and vegetables in record time and went on to demolish what had turned out to be the perfect reinforcer.

Nothing more was said about the transaction. The following week David had to eat six pieces of meat and four forkfuls of beets for another plateful of french fries. I then began very gradually to decrease the amount of french fries and increase the amount of vegetables and meat until a balance was found.

I was so pleased with my results that I decided to try the same tactic on David's brother. I found, much to my dismay, that it didn't work. Then I remembered that Michael was lukewarm about french fries. But he loved ice cream. So there it was! *When* you eat your meat and vegetables, *then* you may have your ice cream.

Snackers and Finicky Eaters

Snackers and finicky eaters have been put together because their problems often have their roots in the same source: numerous references to their eating habits. These children have learned they can get a lot of attention by eating in a way that causes their parents concern. The less said to the children about the problem the better.

If your child snacks instead of eating regular meals, clear out the snack foods in the house. Restrict the amount of money the child has so he can't get snacks as readily. When a child eats a regular meal, then he can have snacks. Otherwise, just serve the regular meal, clear the table after thirty minutes without comment, and ignore whining and complaining. In all likelihood the child will be so hungry in a day he will begin to eat more regularly.

Janet Smith was a fifteen-year-old whose diet consisted principally of pizza after school, popcorn at night, fruit, cereal with lots of sugar and milk on it, and soda. Both her parents had stopped supervising her eating habits closely. Other people such as her grandmother and friends of the family were constantly commenting about her diet.

Finally her parents became concerned over the way she was eating. Her father, a psychologist, instituted a simple program. He asked everyone not to speak to Janet about the way she was eating. He told his daughter that he was worried about her snacking and lack of regular meals, and that henceforth she was to receive no more money for snacks. He also outlawed snack foods in the house. In addition, he told her that when she began to eat more regularly she would be able to get her fall wardrobe.

Janet balked. She ate nothing for dinner that night and nothing for breakfast the next day. In school she reportedly ate her lunch for the first time. At dinner she toyed with her food. Her parents said nothing about it. She ate a little that night and even more the next day. In order to monitor her progress, her father and mother began to eat at home regularly. They got what they wanted: Janet began to eat regular meals. She got what she wanted: her wardrobe, and parents who ate their meals with her.

In the case of a finicky eater, follow the same program. If the child doesn't want to eat, don't make an issue out of it. Let her know that your time isn't infinite and that you cannot always serve the meals exactly as she wants them. She is, however, more than welcome to eat what is available, or she can make other food herself. Let it go at that. After a while, when she is hungry enough, she will learn to eat more foods. If necessary, the program described in the section on underweight can be used too.

Mrs. Dunn had recently remarried, inheriting a ten-year-old daughter and an eight-year-old son along with a husband. The problem was that the children didn't like anything she cooked. They informed her of their food preferences: vegetables were out, bacon and hamburger were acceptable meats, potatoes and noodles were okay, and desserts were their favorites.

Mrs. Dunn felt they were testing her. She told them she appreciated their likes and dislikes and would take them into account when she cooked. On the other hand, she could not be guided solely by what they liked, as four people were concerned with dinner, not just two.

She tried to make dinners as attractive as possible. She also established her policy: no one had to eat anything she made, but she could not run a restaurant and take special orders. She would set the food out, and the children could eat her meal or make whatever they wanted if they preferred. She told them that she would appreciate it if they would give her cooking an honest try. They did and found they liked at least some of it. When they saw they could not manipulate her into serving them only what they wanted, they stopped asking for special dishes.

It was not easy for Mrs. Dunn to take the stand she did, but she figured that in the long run it made the most sense. She believed that the children would eventually come to accept her and her food even if she did not make them special meals. She was right.

Junk Food

You can help a child get over junk food crazes by keeping junk food out of your house *and* reinforcing more nutritious foods. Substitute raisins and nuts or dried fruits for potato chips in a child's lunch box. Carrot sticks and fruit can be left out for a child's snack instead of taco chips and Fritos. Work *with* the child instead of on him. Read the ingredient list of junk food with a child so he or she knows exactly what chemicals are being eaten along with the food itself.

You can also set up a more explicit reinforcement system. Attach a reward to decreases in amounts of junk food eaten.

Overeating

Overweight children tend to become overweight adults. Obese children usually have an oversupply of fat cells, developed through overeating in childhood. The cost of being overweight is a high one, not only in money spent on food, clothing and medically related costs, but also in social prestige and feelings of self-worth.

Some young children have voracious appetites and want to eat everything in sight. To correct this problem, first analyze the situation. Is the child trying to model your behavior? Are you serving too much? Are you allowing too much snacking? With young children you can best solve the problem by setting firm limits. Serve a reasonable portion and nothing more. Eliminate snacks, switch to skim milk, and the problem is half solved. You might have to put up with some whining and crying, but if it is greeted with deaf ears it will soon stop.

Helping older children lose weight and change persistent eating habits is considerably more difficult, but it can be done. It is usually also necessary to get a child to be more active physically so that more calories are burned up.

Do not set up a situation in which you are *making* your child lose weight. That will usually only make him dig his heels in. When it comes right down to it, most overweight children do not like the way they look. During certain close moments they will share that feeling with you. If they have attempted diets before, they undoubtedly feel despair and resignation and are hesitant to fail in yet another diet. They may also be reluctant to enter athletic contests and boy-girl activities. But if you are sympathetic instead of critical, you can probably enlist the child's cooperation.

Let's examine the steps involved in instituting a behavioral weight-loss program. They can all be put in the framework of the three-step method: specify goals, intervene, evaluate.

There are eight to ten steps in a behavior weight-loss program. (Steps 9 and 10 are optional.)

1. Set a weight-loss goal. If you think a child is more than fifteen percent overweight, work out a target with a physician. Write down the child's actual weight and the target weight on a piece of graph paper.
2. Weigh the child each week and record and graph his weight.
3. Plan the child's food intake with a view toward reduction of the number of calories. Serve accordingly.
4. Teach the child how and what to eat.
5. Model the behavior you want. Eat small portions of the same things.
6. Keep a food diary with the child and record his caloric intake.
7. Have the child participate in an exercise program.
8. Tie reinforcers to weight loss, and give them to the child when the agreed-upon weight loss occurs.
9. Reinforce yourself (with a new hat or a fishing pole) when the child has met a specific goal.
10. Deprive yourself of a privilege if the weight-loss goal is not met.

Let us now examine how to implement the above steps.

1. *Set a goal.* Allow plenty of time for the weight-loss target to be met. The trouble with crash diets is that habits really aren't changed, so the weight goes back on. There are no magic solutions here. It takes patience and work.

2. *Weigh the child* at the same time each week, preferably before breakfast. See that he or she is wearing approximately the same amount

of clothing (if any), and use the same scales. A popular system of record-keeping is this one:

Date	3/1	3/8	3/15	3/22
Weight	101	99	96	94

Record-keeping is essential in this kind of program. Make a deal with yourself—no record-keeping, no complaining. The child should see this record, although it does not have to be publicly posted.

3. *Plan the child's food intake* with a view toward caloric reduction and serve accordingly. Start by regulating the portions you serve. Get the child used to eating small portions. Use one pat of butter over the potatoes—or none at all—instead of a few tablespoons. If it will help, use a measured amount for each serving. However, don't go overboard at the beginning and serve tiny amounts. Reduce portions gradually.

Snack foods especially should be curtailed. Keep on hand plenty of diet soda and pieces of cut-up carrots or celery. Cut down on the amount of salt on food, both in the preparation and in the serving. The simpler and blander the food, the less incentive there will be to eat it for its taste.

If you are not home for meals, grandparents, domestic workers, babysitters and so forth should be aware of your goals and given instructions to work with the youngster as you would.

4. *Teach the child how, when and what to eat.* Train the child to eat more slowly. Overweight children (and adults too) eat so fast that their brain and stomach fail to coordinate; they take in more than they require. Have the youngster swallow what is in his mouth *before* he puts the next portion on his fork. Better yet, have the child actually place his fork down between bites. As a matter of course, require that five or preferably ten minutes go by before you serve seconds.

Most overweight children are in the habit of eating every single thing on their plates, even if they are not hungry. Help your child break that habit. This is especially important if you eat out frequently. Let him know that it is not really wasteful in the long run to discard that extra bit of food.

Train your child to delay gratification with food too. Require a five-minute wait between his announced urge for a snack and the actual preparation of the snack. If five minutes seems too long, then begin with a shorter period of time, but start someplace. And be sure the snack is non-fattening.

Train the child to eat in one place—at the kitchen table or at the dining-room table. Help him break the habit of unconscious eating—that is, eating while watching TV, consuming leftovers while stacking dishes, nibbling while talking, or automatically opening the refrigerator door as soon as he comes home from school. Require and reinforce the child's sitting down to eat and being aware of what he is doing.

5. *Model the behavior you want.* It is hard to eat a salad while watching someone else gobble down french fries. You might have to diet too.

Prepare to spend more time at the table. Placing a fork down between bites takes more time than gobbling food. Expect your meals to last longer, and stay around to keep the youngster company. Show him how to eat slowly. Don't put a lot of salt on your food if you expect him to eat bland food.

6. *If possible, keep the food diary with the child,* not for him. The more you work on the problem together, the easier it will be to solve. An abbreviated eating diary might look like this:

	M	T	W	Th	F	S	Sun
Breakfast							
Snack							
Lunch							
Snack							
Supper							
Snack							
TOTAL							

7. *Have the child exercise every day.* The more "natural" these exercises are, the better, for the child will be gaining social skills as well as interests. Bicycle riding, hiking, swimming, and playing ball are preferable to doing calisthenics. But many overweight children find it difficult to participate in sports, and there is no point in forcing them. Exercises will burn off excess calories, and that will probably hasten the day when the child will be willing to engage in more social

and active sports. You can adapt the exercises from the *Royal Canadian Air Force Book of Exercises* or any elementary-school physical education manual.

8. *Tie a reward to the above behaviors.* In fact, reinforce everything the child does right. Plan incentives with the child. Make the criteria for obtaining the rewards crystal clear. This can be facilitated by accurate record-keeping. If there are difficult areas, they will stand out like the proverbial sore thumb. You will then be able to examine the problem more clearly and change the kind of food that is available in the house, the rewards, the way food is served, or whatever is the stumbling block.

One record that parents have found quite helpful follows.

Date________________

Behavior	Met Criteria?	Reward
Completed exercises	Y N	
Had food left over	Y N	
Put down utensils between bites	Y N	
Delayed seconds by five minutes	Y N	
Ate only at table	Y N	
Delayed between asking for and getting snack	Y N	
Had only low-calorie snacks	Y N	
Ate fewer calories than targeted aim	Y N	

This chart, plus the eating diary and the weekly weigh-in, will give you all the information you need to successfully follow a sound program.

Focus on the positive things your child does. Conversely, do not make any disparaging remarks, no matter how oblique, about your child's ungainly appearance or excess weight. A fat child knows he is fat. He needs encouragement, not criticism.

Slip in some extra rewards—rewards that were not contracted for—every once in a while. Clothes are perfect in this regard, especially something that you think will make your child feel more attractive. Boys usually love boots (construction worker boots, snowmobile boots, hiking boots and so forth) and sneakers. Girls' tastes tend to be more all-encompassing. The simple words "You've been looking so (handsome) (pretty) lately that I thought these ____________ would look terrific on you" can go a long way toward giving your child a new self-image, one that he or she will be willing to work for.

9. *Reinforce yourself.* Helping your child lose weight requires work. It is also one of the most important things you can do for him. When you have done a good job, reward yourself as well as the youngster. Buy yourself that new dress or fishing pole that you always wanted. Make its purchase contingent on an explicit weight loss. Motivation works for adults as well as children.

10. *Impose sanctions on yourself.* Step 10, like step 9, is optional, but it can serve as the voice of conscience if you are tempted to "cheat" by serving fattening foods, skipping over details in teaching your child how to eat, and so forth. For example, you can announce publicly, "If there are no low-calorie snacks available tomorrow, I'll give five dollars to the political candidate I hate most." That's usually enough to get a person moving.

You might have to tinker around with the program just described. But if you are conscientious about your record-keeping and use the reinforcers, you should reach long-lasting success.

The Underweight Child

If a child is grossly underweight, it makes sense to check his condition with a physician. Vitamins and medication might be needed as well as training. For training, use the three-step method.

1. *Specify.* First, establish an ideal weight. Mark the actual weight of the child on the left-hand side of a piece of graph paper and the target weight on the right. Your goal is to increase the youngster's weight and her consumption of nutritious foods. The record forms earlier in this chapter can easily be adapted for this purpose.

2. *Intervene.* The second step is to reinforce eating and weight gain. This can best be accomplished by listing all the child's favorite foods, toys and activities, choosing the ones that you think would be most effective as reinforcers, and tying them to eating more and gaining weight.

3. *Monitor.* Monitoring can best be accomplished by weighing the child each week and keeping records of the amounts and kinds of food consumed. When you weigh the child, you should record the weight in the appropriate column on a graph.

The following case study will show how such a program can operate. Stan Carter, a seven-year-old, was placed on a behaviorally oriented program because he ate only a few foods and was grossly underweight. A weekly target was set: a weight gain of one pound and the eating of two new foods.

After observing Stan, his parents decided that watching TV in the evening and playing outside with friends after school were his favorite activities. They also knew he desperately wanted a two-wheeler (which they had been prepared to buy him). They decided to use these three things as reinforcers. In keeping with Stan's love of games, they also decided to make the eating of new foods into a game.

Stan's parents told him that to help keep track of new foods eaten they would make up a color-coded menu. Mrs. Carter made a list of foods that were brownish in color, such as pancakes, hamburgers, chocolate milk, toast, sausages and so forth. Another list was made of foods that were greenish in appearance, such as spinach, broccoli, lettuce and so forth. Yellowish foods (bananas, corn, lemon jello, etc.) were then listed, as well as foods that were white, purple, red and orange in appearance.

The reason for the parents' concern—Stan's health—was made explicit, and the target was set: one food of each color at each meal (three colors a meal was established as the goal). For example, if rice (white) and hamburgers (brown) were served, Stan could choose one food from the yellow category or the green category. They let Stan choose what was to be served as much as possible, because they knew that choice can facilitate cooperation. At the beginning one tablespoon was considered sufficient, although later this amount was increased. To help build up his appetite, snacks were restricted.

Stan was informed he could play outside until four o'clock each day, provided he ate all the required foods. On days he ate a new food, he was allowed to play outside until five-thirty and could even watch an extra TV program. In addition he was informed he would get his two-wheeler when he had put on fifteen pounds.

Stan began to eat new foods. The first night or two he gagged over the vegetables, but his parents wisely ignored this. The first few days, snacks were not given at all. Later, popcorn with lots of melted butter was served during TV time as a reward for having eaten all three meals satisfactorily. Within two months Stan had eaten nineteen different foods and found he liked a number of them. He had also earned his bicycle, which he had picked out of a catalogue when the program started. Being underweight was never a problem again for this child.

Good Eating Habits and Independence

Children have to learn about balanced diets. Parents can facilitate the learning by letting a child practice choosing a balanced diet. A child cannot learn this lesson in one day, but over the years he should become aware of the importance of vitamins and minerals, the basic seven food groups and the necessity of following simple health rules.

One effective way of promoting this knowledge is to have the child help you shop; this will give him practice in making decisions about food. When taking a child shopping, you might say, for example: "We have to pick foods today that will give us vitamins and minerals so we will be strong. We have to choose today from among these groups: green vegetables, proteins, starches, and fruit. Will you help?" After the fruit has been chosen, ask the youngster to help choose the vegetables. Ask which ones she likes best. Ask how she would like them prepared, so that all of the ingredients can be bought at one time.

If the child replies that she doesn't like vegetables, you have to acknowledge her feelings as real, but explain that because of health reasons *everyone* (remember the importance of modeling here) has to eat *some* foods from each group. Make it clear that health is not a matter of whim. Explain that no one has to eat a lot of the foods in question, just enough to meet the basic health requirements. Explain which foods can substitute for each other. Be as flexible as you can, and then you'll have the right to expect that behavior from the youngster. Reinforce trying. Let your child know that everyone has likes and dislikes when it comes to food, but that it is better if these likes and dislikes are based on experimentation rather than appearance or imagination. The more the child tries, the more likely she is to find a sufficient number of likes to manage a balanced diet.

When you take a youngster shopping, you have to know how to say "no." Be consistent. If the answer is "no," tell the child the reason why and then refer back to the reason. For example, you might say, "We can't buy steak this week because we haven't budgeted for it." The next time all you have to do is say: "That's not in our budget this week" and let it go at that. If the answer is "no" for nutritional reasons, let her know that too and tell her what would be acceptable.

The more children participate in the planning of meals and shopping, the more likely it is that they will eat what is served. And remember that everyone is entitled to his own taste. Most children think TV dinners are superior to gourmet food, and they are entitled to that opinion, just as you are entitled to yours.

With just a little bit of help, many ten- and eleven-year-old children are capable of doing the family shopping. You have to train them to use a list, but the efforts are worth it—they will develop feelings of competence and you will receive a great deal of help.

Children eventually have to learn to become self-sufficient in the kitchen. They will learn this quite readily if you teach them one step at a time. As always, start small. Let the child prepare his own cold cereal. Insist that he clean up after himself. The ripe old age of two or three is none too early to start. Even preschoolers can learn how to make cinnamon toast or pop frozen waffles in the toaster. You'll have to supervise at first, but they'll learn quickly, especially if they are motivated by the fact that you won't do it for them. Always let children know that privileges entail responsibilities too. Do *not* clean up any messes—take the time to get the ones who made them to do it. Make the rules clear, and then enforce and reinforce them.

Children can also help in the preparation of tuna or egg salad at an early age. The first time a child is allowed to turn on the burner by himself—under supervision, of course—should be a big occasion. Reward him by letting him know how pleased you are and giving him extra privileges. Teach a child to make popcorn and he'll love the privilege of being able to cook.

By the time a child is nine or ten she should be almost self-sufficient in the kitchen. Of course it helps if you prepared your child for this by having her help you wash dishes, clean up, prepare Jell-O, make cakes and so forth. Once children can manage in the kitchen, they are well on their way to independence—and so are you.

In summary, the following techniques have been found to be effective in building good eating habits:

1. Keep to a regular schedule for meals.
2. Make portions small.
3. Make meals attractive.

4. Ignore crying, wheedling and whining about food.
5. If your child does not eat enough, eliminate snacking and foods that contain sugar.
6. Make your attention contingent on appropriate behavior.
7. Set food out for thirty minutes. Clear the dishes away then, without comment, if your child has not eaten.
8. Share responsibility.
9. Observe Grandma's Law.
10. Make changes gradual.
11. Reinforce all the good things a child does.

The following procedures have been found to be ineffective and even harmful:

1. Nagging.
2. Hollering at or threatening a child.
3. Doing things for a child that he can do for himself.
4. Coaxing and pleading with a child to eat.
5. Allowing a child to eat between meals when she has special problems.
6. Ridiculing a child.

If you work at it, eating does not have to be a problem for you and your child.

CHAPTER VI

Toilet Training

Many parents don't mind changing diapers at all. They feel that their children will "catch on" to toilet training, and at about three years most children do toilet-train themselves. Other parents would rather dispense with diapers as early as possible, but hesitate to do so because of a fear that early training is harmful to children. It is simply a myth that early toilet training leads to emotional problems. The vast majority of children who have been toilet-trained early do not show any evidence of emotional problems. The age at which toilet training starts is less important than the method used. The behavior modification approach is a positive as well as an easy method. Once a child is physiologically ready, training can be accomplished in a day or two, if you are prepared to make them full days. Or you can do it more gradually.

Toilet training is messier than most of the jobs a parent has to do, but it is not so complex or so complicated as a lot of others. There is sometimes a great deal of emotional involvement, which can hinder teaching, but the number of teaching goals you have to set is limited. The two primary goals at the beginning of toilet training are teaching a baby to use a potty or toilet and teaching her to tell you when she needs to use it. Later, children need to learn to go by themselves, to use outside toilets, to hold back urine or feces when no toilet is available, and to sleep through the night without wetting. Each of these behaviors can be taught through the three-step method. But first let's talk about readiness and what can be done even before a child is "ready."

Readiness for toilet training comes about when nerve connections mature and the youngster gains control over the sphincter muscles. Elimination is initially an involuntary action. What goes in has to come out, and the child has no control over it. In addition, the bladder and bowels are so small they cannot contain waste products for any length of time. As the youngster ages, he or she develops more storage room and better muscle control. The child can begin to control defecation and urination, just as he or she can control the movement of arms and fingers. Most children evolve a more or less regular time for bowel movements. When muscle control and regularity have developed and the organ is of sufficient size, the child is "ready" for training. This is more a physiological process than a psychological one. In most cases readiness occurs before the child's second birthday. The average baby is ready at about sixteen months.

Bowel Training

The first part of training consists of teaching the baby the vocabulary that will eventually become part of a signaling system. When cleaning up the baby you might say, "Baby made a duty now" (using whatever term you want to use for elimination). Keep on repeating the word in its proper context so that it becomes a part of the child's vocabulary.

Another active step a parent can take is to get the youngster a potty. Use this potty even before regularity develops in order to get the baby used to and comfortable with it. Make it a proud day when you give the child the potty. Communicate to the baby that it is her very own possession. The child's bedroom is often a good place to keep the potty, as usually there are enough toys and books there to keep the child occupied while both of you are waiting.

Let the child get used to the potty at her own speed. Let her explore how it is constructed. Without prodding she will eventually find that it makes a comfortable seat. That is at least half the battle. It's all right if the youngster is wearing clothes during this exploration; she can always learn how to take off enough clothes for toileting later.

A potty chair rather than an adult toilet seat is recommended for training. First, the potty is close enough to the ground that the child will not worry about falling or being trapped on the seat. In addition, children will not worry that they might get flushed down the toilet. Toilet training and worrying do not make a good combination. Besides, the potty seat fits, so waiting is relatively pleasant.

Let the child know that his or her potty is akin to the toilet that Mommy and Daddy use and that it is used in the same way. This doesn't mean that an adult has to always have the child as an audience, but occasionally watching an adult can be helpful to a child.

While the child is learning the vocabulary and getting used to the potty, look for signs of readiness. The signs are (1) a diaper that is dry for a few hours; (2) an indication by the child that he or she is uncomfortable with a full diaper; and (3) an indication by the child that he or she is aware of toileting needs (for example, a child may begin to pull at his diaper).

In a while, a more or less set time for elimination will appear (often after breakfast). That is the most obvious sign of readiness. Often this regularity is accompanied by silence, a certain look in the child's eye or even a grunt. Each child has his own way of telling you that he needs to eliminate. A parent has to observe closely what sign his child is using and capitalize on this information. Later it will be important to help make a signal for toileting explicit and to use it *before* eliminating.

Children develop their own way of doing things, and where possible respect this. Some children, for example, prefer to be naked during this time. Others like to wear their socks or a shirt, and that's fine too. Some children prefer company, while others prefer privacy.

Make sure the child is playing near the potty when you think it's time for him to have a bowel movement. Then place him on the potty. Reward his sitting on the potty with lots of praise and smiles and hugs. The idea of course is to seat, not force, a child. While he is there, entertain him by reading him a story or talking to him. If he gets up, don't force the issue. Try to get him back, but if that doesn't work, discontinue your story or talking and let him know as best you can that you'll continue when he's sitting down again. If he moves his bowels away from the potty, try again next time. If he moves his bowels in the potty, let him know how pleased you are. Make the compliment strong and your delight overt. Show how proud you are of his accomplishments by telling everyone what a big boy he is or what a big girl she is.

Food can speed up the process of getting the child to use the potty appropriately. Reserve something special that your child loves, such as cereal bits, raisins or bits of dried fruit. When the child uses the potty appropriately, give him some food and tell him that the next time he uses the potty he'll get some cereal or fruit. The word "reserve" is used advisedly. Using food rewards indiscriminately, other than for important areas of training, tends to devalue them as rewards.

After a few days of success, get the child training pants as well as a special toy that only big girls (or boys) can have. Let her know how proud you are that she has graduated to training pants and tell her you imagine she feels even prouder than you do. Take her on a special trip and let her know that she can go on that trip now because she knows how to use a potty, that little children couldn't go on that trip. And by all means keep on praising whenever she does things right.

After the child has mastered the potty, it's time to work on signaling. To get him to signal to you systematically when he needs to go, try the following procedures.

1. *Specify* your goal: To teach the child to signal.

2. *Intervene.* When you take him to the potty, say, "It's time to potty. What is it time to do now? Say 'potty.'" The aim is to get him to answer your cue with the word potty. When he says it, reinforce him with approval.

When he has finished, ask him what he did. If he can't answer, say it for him. Then ask him again. If he still can't answer, whisper the answer in his ear, and then have him say it. Make a big deal out of his being able to do that. Work on this routine until he can say the word without your having to use the cue, "Say potty." When the child can answer your question without the cue, he knows what the word refers to.

After a while, pretend you've forgotten what it's time to do. Ask for the child's help. Make it into a game. Say, "I forget—is it time to get dressed? No. Is it time to go to the park?" and so on. Somewhere along the line the child will probably get the idea. If not, go back to previous cues.

As time goes on, phase out your cues and gradually leave more of the responsibility to the child. Praise signaling lavishly, and your child will soon learn how to do it.

3. *Evaluate.* Keep a calendar chart and check off each time he signals.

(This same system can also be used to teach a child how to signal when it is time to urinate.)

Very often bowel training is as simple as that. The main thing is to keep your child near the potty when you think it's time for him to go, watch carefully for the signal, and reward liberally. You can also make trips to the park, visits with friends and so forth part of that routine. When Mary moves her bowels, then she goes to the park. (It isn't advisable to use this contingency until you are reasonably sure the child moves her bowels with regularity. And not every child moves her bowels every day either.)

Occasionally there are children who are bowel-trained all at once—once they know the rules of the game they almost never have an accident. But that is rare. When accidents do happen, remember how undeveloped a child's muscles really are. Even when a child has an accident and informs you after the fact, praise him for letting you know what happened. Let him know how much more comfortable he will be if he lets you know beforehand, and how proud you are of his ability to communicate.

Sometimes "accidents" don't seem quite so accidental—that is, the child will get off the potty and then have her bowel movement. When that happens, express mild disappointment, clean her up (if she's old enough she should help), and let it go at that. Let her know that she can earn a reward for using the potty, and try again the next day. The idea will sink in eventually.

Setbacks will occur more often if your child feels that she can control your emotional state. If you react with horror or dismay to an accident, the child may feel she has you where she wants you. If you take these things in stride, they will disappear rather quickly, particularly if the emphasis is on what the child does right. An accident is only an accident, and everyone gets toilet-trained sooner or later. Don't judge the worth of your child by the rapidity and completeness of her toilet training. Just continue to make your expectations clear, and be lavish in your reinforcement of the right things. Do not induce shame and self-disgust. They are too heavy a burden for a child to bear. Instead, try to get your child to want to be clean and orderly by letting her know how pleased you are when her pants are dry.

As the child develops, she will discover that she can retain her stool for longer and longer periods of time. Most children delight in the sense of mastery they begin to feel. Like any new skill, they will practice it over and over again. This can result in spending a long time on the potty, and to a busy parent it can be exasperating. Power struggles sometimes develop around this time. Better to delight with your child at her new-found skill. Let her know that you too are proud of what she is capable of doing. At the same time, you can explain that you're busy and will be back as soon as she's finished. Let her know that a surprise treat is in store for her when she has finished, and when she has fulfilled her part of the bargain, fulfill yours.

More formal incentive systems can also be used for toilet-training problems. John Smith was three years old. He was continually constipated. Usually he moved his bowels only once a week. Bowel movements were often induced by medication. His mother often had him sit on the toilet one or two hours a day. She tried to comfort him while he was on the toilet, but this didn't seem to help. He was finally treated by a psychologist, who used the three-step method.

1. *Specify.* The goal was to get the child to move his bowels by himself more regularly.

2. *Intervene.* The intervention program the psychologist recommended was to induce the bowel movement without medication. The father was to tell his son that he was leaving the room and would return when his son had defecated in the toilet. When he had used the toilet, then he could play in the tub with some of his toy boats. Each day he used the toilet appropriately he was to receive a gold star. When he had earned three gold stars he could turn them in for a new toy boat. If the child called the father in without having used the toilet, the father was instructed to repeat the rules to the boy and leave immediately. The father never had to invoke that rule. The boy began to use the toilet appropriately, and the constipation disappeared.

3. *Evaluate.* The father checked off on a calendar each time the child had a bowel movement and counted up the gold stars.

Even chronic soiling can be treated through behavior modification, although it is strongly urged that the child who chronically soils be checked by a physician, as soiling can be caused by organic problems as well as constipation or faulty training methods. One eight-year-old girl was treated for soiling by a combination of time-out and rewards. If the girl showed evidence of soiling, she was sent to her room. This cut the soiling in half. When she was allowed to skip washing the dishes if she had clean underwear, the soiling practically disappeared.

Even the most stubborn children can be taught bowel mastery if the parent is persistent and positive. Once a bowel-training program has been undertaken, stick with it. Being wishy-washy helps no one.

(If for some reason you want to accelerate the process and are prepared to spend a day or two doing little but toilet training, an excellent book for the purpose is Nathan H. Azrin and Richard M. Foxx's *Toilet Training in Less Than a Day.*)

Bladder Control Training

Bladder control usually develops later than bowel control. The average baby's bladder becomes large enough to retain urine for a one- or two-hour period at about eighteen months. If a child wakes up dry from a nap, there are no physiological reasons that will interfere with toilet training. The same process—reinforcement—is used in both bladder training and bowel training. Since urination is considerably more frequent than defecation, you might have to remind the child to use the potty more frequently, but you also have more of an opportunity to reinforce appropriate behavior.

The following case study describes how one family trained their daughter to use the potty for urination.

The Nolan family had a chance to take an extended automobile trip but were hesitant to go because their sixteen-month-old daughter Jane was still in diapers. On the other hand, they felt that their daughter was ready for training, since she usually woke up dry from her nap, even after drinking a large glass of juice before falling asleep.

Mrs. Nolan felt it was worth trying to train her daughter. Every hour or so she placed Jane on the potty and insisted that Jane stay on the potty until she urinated. As a result, Jane was frequently in tears and began to develop an aversion to the potty.

Mrs. Nolan discussed the problem with her pediatrician. Together they worked out a different kind of program. They agreed that Mrs. Nolan would not force Jane to use the potty. Instead, potty sitting was to be made as enticing as possible. Mrs. Nolan was to read to Jane and play games with her when she was on the potty. If Jane got tired and wandered off, Mrs. Nolan was to stop reading and/or playing with her. When Jane returned to the potty, the story or game would continue. Every time Jane urinated in the potty, Mrs. Nolan was to give her a reward and praise her lavishly.

The program started the next day when Jane awoke dry from a nap. Mrs. Nolan assumed that Jane's bladder was full then and that that would be a good time to place her on the potty. Jane was told she could have some dried fruit after she used the potty. Mrs. Nolan also read to Jane from her favorite book while she was sitting. Jane was allowed to leave the potty whenever she wanted to, but when she did, her mother stopped reading. When Jane returned, she continued. Whenever she used the potty she was given many hugs and kisses along with the dried fruit.

Before suppertime Jane used the potty four more times. She received eight pieces of fruit altogether. After supper Jane was given training pants and told that only "big" girls could wear them. Mr. and Mrs. Nolan also rewarded their daughter with food and trinkets for having dry pants. When the grandparents came over that evening they were told, in a dramatic way, that their granddaughter was well on her way to being toilet-trained, and what a big girl she was.

The following day, Jane was put on the potty every hour and a half after voiding. This time they used sips of iced tea as the reward for having dry pants. The iced tea not only reinforced Jane's attempts to keep her pants dry, it also increased the frequency of her urinating. She then had even more opportunities to be rewarded for going to the potty, and her parents had more opportunities to reward her. When Jane had an accident, her parents mildly reproached her by letting her know they considered her too big for that. They were also slow to change her, as they wanted her to feel a mild discomfort. They had Jane help with the changing as best she could. They gave positive reinforcement, however, much more frequently than negative.

By the third day Jane was no longer having accidents. Since the eventual goal was to have Jane go by herself, she was informed she would receive an extra bit of fruit if she signaled an adult before she had to use the potty. That afternoon, Jane told her father she wanted to go. She received her dried fruit as well as hugs and kisses and exclamations of how proud everyone was of her. She gave that signal three times that day. By the fourth day the Nolans were satisfied that Jane was completely toilet-trained. They continued to use food and trinkets as rewards for the next few days. At the end of the week they phased out the food rewards and substituted games. They continued to explicitly praise Jane, however, and told everyone who would listen how proud they were of their daughter.

The Nolans were able to take their automobile trip, and during that five-day period there were no accidents.

Routines as well as consequences can be helpful in toilet training. When my son David was two, I was under the pressure of a deadline and wanted to speed up the toilet training. Knowing that David usually had a bowel movement after breakfast, I decided to capitalize on his regularity. I also noted that David would wet his pants during the day. David often played so hard he would forget to go inside and would wind up wetting his pants, or he would wait so long he would have to make a mad dash to the bathroom, trying to hold it in. Sometimes he made it to the bathroom and sometimes he didn't.

I established two routines for David. First, he had to move his bowels in the morning *before* he went outside to play. Second, he had to stay inside for twenty minutes if he wet his pants. David had one accident outside, and I followed through with the consequences. This turned out to be the next to last accident David had. I told my wife about the training program, and she followed the same rules. David had only one more accident after that, and then he was fully toilet-trained.

The most frequent problem encountered in daytime training is wetting during play. The problem is essentially one of timing. Many small children become so engrossed in play that they find it difficult to break off what they are doing. This is best handled by structuring the child's schedule so that he has to interrupt what he is doing to come inside. Keep a record of his urinating schedule and base your calling him in on that. Explain to the child very directly what you are doing and why. Tell him he is too old to keep wetting his pants and he'll be able to play much better if he is dry. Let him know that when he can come in by himself you won't have to do it for him. He might balk at the idea of being called in all the time (a whistle is sometimes easier than having to shout), but explain that it is not a matter for him to decide. Every time he uses the toilet, let him know how proud you are and remind him how much more comfortable he is. Place a gold star or some other check mark in his room. Tell him that he can earn a gold star each day he's dry. When he gets five or ten gold stars, he can go on that special trip or get that toy he's wanted for so long.

Another common problem is difficulty in using unfamiliar toilets. Prevention is the best cure here. Have the child get used to different toilets even during training. If you are using a potty, occasionally place the youngster on the big toilet. Get him used to going other places, even outdoors, before he becomes too set in his habits.

If it is too late for a preventive program, bear with the child and tell him you know that it is difficult but everyone has to get used to going in different places. Use the power of suggestion. Run water and tell the child that when he's ready he'll go. Use an incentive as well as encouragement in the beginning. Give the youngster plenty of liquids to make it easier.

Nighttime Training

Most young children continue to wet the bed at night even after they have achieved daytime control. This is largely a function of a small bladder that cannot retain urine for a long period and a sphincter muscle that will respond to weak urges. If the bladder is too small, all your efforts will be futile. If a child is wet all the time during the night, it isn't even worth trying. If, on the other hand, he is dry after long naps or only wets once or twice during the night, you can save a lot of laundry and make everyone's life easier by picking him up and taking him to the bathroom at night. Usually, somewhere between the ages of two and three, children develop to the point where they can sleep through the night without wetting.

When you pick up a youngster at night to take him to the toilet, it is usually not desirable to wake him. He can do everything while half asleep. Waking him might hasten toilet training (although there is no evidence for this), but it is apt to create a sleep problem, as many children find it difficult to fall asleep after having been wakened.

The best time to take a child to the bathroom at night is just before the adults go to bed. Most parents help a child go through all the motions of toileting; a better way is called graduated guidance. In the graduated guidance method only the minimum physical pressure needed to get the child through all of the essential steps in toileting is used. In other words, do not carry the child to the toilet. Instead, walk along with him until he reaches the toilet. Do not pull the child's pants down, but place his hands in the proper place and get him started. As soon as the child begins to go through the correct motions of walking, undressing or assuming a position convenient to elimination—*no matter how slightly*—reduce your guidance and let the child take over. That way the guidance is never so strong that it resembles physical coercion, nor do you ever replace the child's initiative.

What do you do if the child continues to wet the bed past age three? As with most bladder problems, it is best to check first with a physician, for too frequent urination and wetting the bed at night can be symptomatic of low-grade bladder infections, and you will want to rule this out before starting any training program.

Training the child to "hold it in" is the most effective way to cure bedwetting (and too frequent urination during the day as well). The training has to be done during the day, of course, but teaching the child to hold it in or empty the bladder only when it is full serves to stretch the bladder. It enables the child to ignore weak urges to urinate so he or she can sleep through the night without voiding, which is a more sensible goal than having the child wake up in the middle of the night to go to the bathroom. Reinforcement is geared to holding back the urine during the day. The method is good for children from three to adolescence.

First, instruct the child to let you know each time he has to void. Jot down the time of each urination. During this period encourage the child to drink as much liquid as he wants. You should also decide on a reinforcer at this time—cookies, trinkets, gold stars that can be exchanged for something the child values, or whatever else will work.

After a day or two of keeping records, ask the child to "hold it in" for two or three minutes past his announced urge to urinate. At the beginning, "holding it in" is difficult. It can be helpful to divert the child during this time by playing some kind of special game, having a discussion or asking a question. Tell the child he will earn his reward when he can hold it in for two or three minutes. If the child cannot tell time, announce that if he can hold it until the big hand gets to the three or whatever, he will get his reward.

When that particular time demand becomes easy for the child to meet, gradually increase it. It helps to keep a record of how long the child can wait, and increase the limit very gradually. In about two weeks the child will probably be able to hold it in for thirty to forty-five minutes past the first cue he receives. Then he will urinate three to five times a day instead of the six or seven times a day that most accident-prone children do.

As your child gets more adept at holding it in, instruct him or her to stop urinating and hold it back for a few seconds during the middle of urination. This strengthens the sphincter muscle and gives a child more control over his bodily functions. Again, be quite lavish in your praise and rewarding of this control. Let the child know how much he is helping himself by learning how to stay dry.

Being able to hold back urine during the day usually transfers to being able to hold it back during sleep. This is not a conscious action on the part of the person. The bladder has stretched from the holding-it-in exercises, and the sphincter muscle does not respond so readily to weak urges. During the night the urges to urinate are weaker than during the day, because the body manufactures less urine during sleep. That is why most people can retain urine in their body for eight hours during the evening but could not wait that long to urinate during the day.

You have nothing to lose, though, by setting up an incentive system for staying dry during the night. Give the child a reward when she meets the target of a specified number of successive dry nights. If bedwetting has been chronic, let the child choose the reward at the beginning of the program. If you are working on less frequent voiding during the day and less frequent accidents, give the child the reinforcer when that target is met. You can know when the target has been met by recording each dry night on a chart:

M	T	W	Th	F	S	Sun
Dry	Dry	Wet	Dry	Dry		

Conditioning devices can also be used to cure bedwetting. They are entirely safe, cause no pain whatever and are quite effective. Urine creates a short circuit in the apparatus, and a buzzer goes off. Some models even switch on the light at the same time. They operate by causing the child to wake when the sphincter muscle in the bladder releases. This strengthens the signaling system from the bladder to the brain.

The first few times the devices are used, children are slow to respond to the signal. Usually a good-sized puddle has been created by the time a child gets out of bed to go to the toilet. But soon a child will begin to respond faster and faster to the signal, and only a drop or two will escape before the youngster is out of bed. Finally, the pressure on the bladder will be sufficient to wake the youngster and he will "beat the bell." Most children learn to get up by themselves within two weeks. It is recommended that you let the child drink a lot of water during the training—this also serves to stretch the bladder directly.

You can use the conditioning apparatus in conjunction with the incentive system and the bladder stretching exercises.

Keep the following points in mind when working on this problem. Work *with* your child, not *on* him. Let him know that a conditioning device is being used to help him, not to punish him. Stress how nice it is that such things exist nowadays. Make your attitude very positive. Explain its operation and test it out in front of him. Rig it up (the directions are quite explicit and easy to follow) and test it out with some water so you'll both know how it operates.

If you use a conditioning device, there will be a lot less fuss if the child is in a room by himself so that his brothers' or sisters' sleep isn't disturbed. If that's not possible, ask everyone to bear with the disturbance, because the problem can usually be solved in about two weeks.

Even though the conditioning usually takes less than two weeks, it pays to keep the device rigged up awhile longer. Occasionally children relapse, so you want to make sure the habit is really instilled. An incentive system should be used in conjunction with this device. Make the special reward contingent on longer and longer periods of dryness, first setting a target at one week, then two weeks and so forth.

Drug therapy has been used with mixed success with bedwetters. Drugs, of course, have to be administered by a physician. Relapse rates have proven to be discouragingly high with drugs, and caution should be used before instituting a program of this type.

Some Additional Problems Concerning Elimination

Preoccupation with waste products is a phase that most children go through. Two-year-olds have an almost uncanny eye for spotting animal feces and will do their best to draw everyone's attention to it. Similarly, children around that age will want to visit everyone's bathroom. These interests usually occur around the time that toilet training is being stressed in the home, and the interest is usually little more than a reflection of the importance of the task they are trying to learn. If you don't let it fluster you, the child will soon learn that all living things give off waste products and that animals eliminate outside; moreover, almost every home has a bathroom, and all plumbing is basically the same.

A somewhat more difficult problem is the use of such words as "duty head" and "pp pants," which lots of preschoolers find hilarious —or at least quite valuable in terms of their potential shock value to adults. If it gets past a certain point, treat it the same way as you would cursing or rudeness. Explain to children that many people do not like to hear those words in that context and that you would appreciate their not using them. If they insist on using them, ignore it, or set a consequence like time-out. If reinforcement is used for more appropriate language, the problem will soon disappear.

Sometimes children who have been toilet-trained for a while will regress. The first thing to do is rule out physical illness. Second, look for particular kinds of stress that the child might be going through. If he is being subjected to a lot of stress (a harsh or punitive teacher, for example, or a bully in the school), work with him on solving the problem. If it is something he has to face, the relaxation procedures described in Chapter 4 can be quite helpful. And of course accidents can bring on lots of attention, so be careful of that. Children need a lot of attention, but as parents we have to see that they get it for the right things.

CHAPTER VII

Sleep and Nighttime Problems

A full and peaceful night's sleep is crucial to good health and good spirits. This holds true for adults as well as for children. There is little that is more draining than being kept up all night by a baby and then having to get through the next day. The baby can always sleep during the day, but the adult can't, and it only takes two or three sleepless nights to incapacitate almost anyone. Prevention is better than cure, so you might as well start right away to establish patterns. The goal is to build sleep into a routine, not an occasion for struggle.

You should try to surround sleeping with as much pleasure as possible. Rocking, crooning, massaging and good heartwarming talk (even if the infant can't understand the words, he or she can grasp the intent) can contribute to making bedtime a special time of communication and love. And children, when they are sleeping, are precious—precious to look at and feel and take pride in. And of course *when* you've finished putting the baby to bed, *then* you can get your reward—some time for yourself, and perhaps the chance to be with a special person alone.

From the outset it must be recognized that individuals, and this includes infants, differ greatly in their need for and approach to sleep. There are good sleepers and good ages for sleeping. Some children resist sleep and some welcome it. The only thing you can do is judge your child as an individual. Sleeping schedules are much like height and weight charts. Weight charts give an average, but they don't take your build and skeletal frame into account. Sleeping schedules can serve as a general guide, but they cannot take into account the child's temperament and activity level, or the family's. Every parent has to find the "right" schedule for himself or herself.

Babies' Schedules

You can prevent a lot of problems by watching carefully and setting the right schedule for the child so that she is relatively sleepy when put to bed. You can also prevent a lot of problems by establishing reasonable routines. If you put a child to bed at your convenience and hope he'll fall asleep, or at least be quiet, you can get into difficulty. With infants, it is usually best to respect the patterns the child has evolved and plan your time around his sleeping schedule. You can gradually shift the patterns to meet the needs of the family by lengthening or shortening the naps and/or putting the youngster to bed earlier or later. Although you cannot make a child sleepy any more than you can make a child hungry, you can establish a schedule that meets the child's needs and yours too. Children do not always know how much rest they require. Parents sometimes have to take the lead and be firm in this area.

Here are some general sleep schedule guidelines.

Newborns usually sleep twenty to twenty-two hours a day. The hours an infant sleeps decrease with age; up until a year, most babies take a long morning and afternoon nap and fall asleep right after dinner. Between one and three years of age, most children take an afternoon nap and will sleep from six-thirty or seven P.M. until morning. From age five to age nine, most children go to bed at seven or seven-thirty P.M., and from age nine to age twelve, somewhere around eight-thirty or nine. After age twelve, many children go to bed at ten on school nights and later on weekends. Again, this is a schedule for the "average" child in the "average" family. A particular child may require more or less sleep.

Newborns follow a self-demand schedule. If they are clean and full, they will sleep whenever they can and wake up mostly to eat. Sleep problems at this age go hand in hand with feeding and scheduling problems. Later, social factors become more important.

Get into the habit right away of giving a baby a nap and putting him or her to bed fairly soon after supper. Rocking, cuddling, and singing can and should be a part of the bedtime routine, but it is best to put a baby to bed before he falls asleep so that dependency patterns—the insistence on being held and cuddled before falling asleep—never get a chance to start.

After a baby is on a more or less regular schedule, there may still be times when he or she wakes up crying in the middle of the night. By all means go in and check to see if there is a physical cause, such as hunger, a full diaper, or a pin that has opened. (Of course teething and colicky babies will also cry steadily.) Once you're assured that the baby is healthy, you might want to hold and rock it anyway, but be sure you don't set a pattern for reinforcing crying. When you're convinced that a baby is simply crying to get attention, the moment has come to put him back to bed. Some babies accept this and some don't. If he continues to cry for your attention you have two choices: you can let him cry it out ("conscious ignoring") or you can spoil him. If you wisely decide to let him cry it out, it sometimes helps to cover the windows and the doors with blankets, as this will muffle the sounds. You can also let your neighbors know what's happening so the police don't come to investigate a case of child abuse. The crying is horrendous, but in two or three days even the most stubborn baby will usually get the message and fall into a more regular—and more suitable—sleep pattern.

Bedtimes

As children grow older, bedtime rituals become more and more important. These rituals can be immensely enjoyable to a family, and they can make everything easier besides. Keep the rituals simple. It's important not to overstimulate youngsters before sleep, but something physical, like tickling or letting a child sit on your lap, can be fun. Establish a sequence for you and your child. Work together on putting things away, then cuddle or tickle him, have him get into his pajamas, and when he is in bed read him a story. He will probably ask you to read the same story over and over again and will try to prolong his time with you as much as he can. As long as you're comfortable and the demands are not unreasonable, stay with the child. Children grow up fast, and that kind of time together can be very rewarding. But you have a need for privacy, and the child needs his rest, so at the right moment—and make this into a ritual too—kiss him good night and leave the room, unequivocally.

Many parents create problems for themselves by walking out uncertainly. When the child calls them to come back, they don't know what to do, especially if the tears come. That uncertainty and the trips back reinforce the crying and the calling. You should make it clear that the good-night kiss is the end. If you're consistent, the tears will stop, because the child will realize they won't get him anywhere. But first, of course, anticipate his needs. See that he has his favorite blanket, he has been to the toilet, he has a glass of water by his bedside, and that everything else he legitimately needs has been taken care of.

Some children have more difficulty falling asleep than others. If a youngster can't fall asleep, accept it. Put some toys in her crib and let her play with them. At least she's getting some rest, and you are too. If you find the toys are keeping her up all night, then limit them. You'll have to experiment to find the right balance.

Often simple reassurance works. Tell a child that a lot of people have that difficulty. Let him know that if he just waits quietly for sleep to come to him, it will. Often it helps a child to take a hot bath just before he goes to bed. And of course make sure he is not overstimulated by TV or active games before bedtime. You might even try massaging his temples or rubbing his back.

If he's still not sleepy or relaxed after a hot bath or a back rub, teach him how to let the tension out of his muscles. This can be accomplished by having him flex separate muscle groups. Have him flex his biceps and make a muscle like Popeye the Sailor. Then have him let go of the tension. Ask him to relax his arm and make it like a wet noodle hanging over the side of the pot. If he's too stiff, tell him to flop his arm. Have him tense and then relax his legs, his stomach muscles, and his shoulders. Massage his temples. Show him how he should breathe in and out, in and out, in a monotonous way. Tell him to think about nothing but breathing, and leave the room.

The opposite technique has also been successful: tell the child to stay up as long as he can. Tell him to think about nothing but staying awake and to fight sleep as hard as he can. That has made many a child sleepy. In any event, be sure to wake him up early in the morning so he doesn't drift into a schedule of late to sleep, late to rise.

Naps

Many parents run into napping problems with children somewhere between two and four. Children start to grow out of the afternoon nap but cannot make it until bedtime. Dinnertime is usually when they're the crankiest. On the other hand, if they take a nap, they find it difficult to fall asleep at night. Either way you lose. In the long run the afternoon nap is going to be dispensed with anyway, so my own preference has been to try to live through the difficult dinner hour.

Getting Out of Bed at Night

There comes a time when children learn to climb out of their cribs. Some children do this in the middle of the night and even leave their room and wander around the house. It's important to be quite strict about this. Children can get themselves into serious trouble that way —for example, turning on the gas burner or pouring ammonia on themselves. Some parents place netting over the top of the crib to prevent the child from climbing out. If you use this method, keep a close eye on the child, for some children react very strongly and can become hysterical. The same is true of locking the child in his room. The emotional side effects are probably not worth it. A harness is often easier to use for a young child, but first try a more positive and less drastic approach than restraint.

Often a positive consequence, combined with firmness and a mild form of punishment, works. For example, set up a chart on the child's wall, and each night he stays in bed, color in an X. Let him know that the more X's he earns, the more treats he can have. And be sure to give a reward for each X. If the youngster is in a crib, promise him a big bed when he or she has stayed in the crib ten consecutive nights.

If the child leaves the room, unceremoniously lead him back to his bed, communicate your displeasure, and firmly tell him he can't leave the room. You might also take away one of his toys every time he leaves the room. If that doesn't work, a spanking might be necessary, for greater punishment in the form of injury might result from these night wanderings. Make the punishment immediate, let the child know what it is for, and let him know it will happen again if he leaves his room after bedtime. If you seldom use spankings, a child will learn that it's very important to stay in his bed at night, and after one or two spankings he will conform.

Some children will want to sleep in your bed at night. The easiest way to solve that problem is to tell the child firmly that he has his bed and you have yours, and he can't sleep in your bed. Keep that rule inflexible. It's okay once in a while to have a child snuggle up in bed with you on a Sunday morning, but you have to be up by then and let him in and should not allow him to wake you up.

Mr. and Mrs. Segal had a problem with Anne, who was three. She would come into their bed at two-thirty each night. The first night they put her back three times and finally gave in. The second night they were so tired they didn't even bother to put her back to bed. For a week Anne woke up each night at the same time and crawled into bed with them. Mr. and Mrs. Segal decided to use the three-step method.

The behavior was certainly easy to specify: they wanted Anne to stay in her crib. To reinforce the behavior they bought her a doll to keep her company in bed. Anne could play with the doll the following day only if she stayed in her crib the night before. Anne's parents also decided to discontinue Anne's nap so that by bedtime she would be extremely tired. Whenever she woke up and came into their room, she would be put back with a sharp reprimand. Within a week they had solved the problem.

Nighttime Fears

A child may develop a fear of going to sleep—and particularly a fear of the dark. He may also believe there are bugs in his room, robbers under the bed, or monsters waiting in the closet for him. You might try getting a night light. Place it where it does not cast shadows, as shadows can heighten the fears. Accept the fact, however, that you're trading off one problem for another, for you will probably want to get rid of the night light eventually. You can do that later by gradually diminishing the size of the bulb, placing furniture in such a way that it obstructs the light, moving the light farther and farther away from the bed, and/or setting up a when-then program. Or you can let the child take a flashlight to bed with her.

If you have a pet, consider allowing the animal to sleep in the same room with the child. Dogs are particularly helpful in allaying a child's fears, as you can "instruct" a dog to protect the child from whatever imaginary fears she has. You can also give her an imaginary dog to scare away intruders.

Five-year-olds (and some younger children too) often have bad dreams. Explain carefully to a child who has bad dreams that dreams are different from reality, that they are a kind of make-believe during sleep. Suppose a child is recounting a bad dream in which, say, his nose fell off. You might tell him that you feel bad he had such a scary dream, but of course people's noses don't fall off in real life. Let him know that everyone dreams and that dreams can't hurt us if we know they're make-believe.

It's usually best to have this kind of discussion during the day rather than on the night of the bad dream. Children who wake up at night with bad dreams sometimes aren't really awake. It's often best just to reassure the child he's okay and was only dreaming, then gently encourage him to go back to sleep. Assure him that you're in the next room and within reach. If the child is badly frightened, sit by his bed for a while and soothe him. But don't make it a habit. You have to use judgment, of course, in cases of upset. Be leery about showering a lot of attention on his fears; they could become worse as a result.

If the child is subject to chronic bad dreams or nighttime fears, you should try to find out whether he or she is under any tension that could be avoided. Is he having problems in school or with other children? If so, try to correct these problems. Make sure you're not overstimulating the child or making too many demands on him. If you're having trouble with a spouse, don't argue in front of the child during this time. It's especially scary for children to be awakened at night by intense arguments—they imagine the worst. So if you have to thrash something out, get a babysitter, and do it where the child will not be quite so affected by the arguing. Take a look at the TV he watches or the books he's reading. Are the programs or books too frightening? Is there too much violence and gore? If so, discourage his exposure to these programs or books during this time, especially before bedtime.

If sleep problems are getting to be too much to handle, you can usually receive help from pediatricians or child psychologists. They have had lots of experience with this kind of difficulty and can pass on some helpful and specific advice.

Fears, no matter how ridiculous they might appear to an adult, are real and terrifying to a child, so be as supportive as you can. Let her know you'll be in the living room or wherever to protect her. Try using a little humor too—like bopping a shadow on the nose. And be aware that bad dreams and fears of this sort generally abate in time. (Fear is discussed more fully in Chapter 8.)

Waking Up

Young children tend to wake up very early—too early for most parents. When a child is under six months, you have no choice but to get up and feed her and change her. You don't have to continue that routine indefinitely, however. As soon as you're sure that hunger or wetness is no longer a problem, you can train a child to play alone until a reasonable hour. The technique is relatively simple and very effective.

First, leave some toys in the child's crib at night so she can amuse herself in the morning. In the morning the child will call out as usual; do not respond for three or four minutes. At the end of that time, ring the alarm. Then go in and attend to her. Do the same thing the following day (including putting the toys in the crib). Keep up that routine for a few more days. The child will learn that her parents come to her *after* the alarm rings and not before. That knowledge will encourage her to play with the toys—she will have learned that since calling out before the alarm rings is futile, she might as well amuse herself. The next step is to set the alarm five minutes later. In all probability she will remain quiet and occupied until the alarm goes off. Each day set the alarm a little later, until you have achieved what you consider to be a reasonable schedule.

When a child is capable of feeding and dressing himself, he should be encouraged to do so. Place a glass of milk and a peanut butter and jelly sandwich in the refrigerator. Have him take his own breakfast under your supervision. Later, when the child gets used to that routine, let him open the refrigerator door himself, get his own napkin and so forth while you just watch. Keep on teaching the child, during the day, how to get his own food. Let him know what he can take by himself and what he can't. All you have to do is fade out of the picture more and more, so that if you want to sleep late on a Sunday morning you will be able to do so without having to worry about the child's being able to take care of himself.

With freedom comes responsibility, so the child will also have to learn to put his dishes in the sink, wipe the table and so forth. These have to be taught, and the when-then method is one of the most effective ways to do it. But don't expect the child to learn everything overnight. You will have to do the work with him at first, and let him know that it is important. Guide him through each task step by step. You also have to recognize that you are making a tradeoff of some extra sleep for some extra work, for there will be times when you find spaghetti strewn over the floor, or all the tin cans converted into soldiers and placed in strategic positions throughout the kitchen. Maintain a sense of humor, and again point out to the child what he can and cannot do.

CHAPTER VIII

Fears

A parent can help a child avoid unnecessary fears, but fear cannot wholly be prevented. On the positive side, fear can help a child survive, for it can lead to caution. Fear of depth, for example, has prevented many children from falling off a high surface, and fear of water has kept many from drowning. Fear of approaching objects can prevent a child from running into a busy street, even though she has no realization of the consequences of being hit by a car.

We have all experienced the drawbacks of fear—the inertia, self-doubt and paralysis it sometimes brings. This kind of fear can often be prevented and overcome, although it must be recognized that some children are more susceptible to fear than others and that children differ greatly in the effect that fear has on them.

In order to prevent fears (at least those that are not innate) from developing and to overcome fears, it is helpful to understand how fears come about. Some are learned through simple imitation. The more fears a parent has, the more fears the child is likely to have. And many of those fears will be the same ones. For example, if Marty sees his mother recoil in fright at the sight of lightning or a spider, he will probably react the same way. Who can blame him, since he has learned that lightning and spiders are dangerous and to be feared?

You can't always hide fright, and it is often necessary to teach children to be afraid of things. But if you think some of your fears are not really rational and you don't want your child to pick them up, try to be cool in front of the youngster. At least some of the time it will keep him or her from developing an unnecessary fear.

Inadequate understanding—and sometimes inadequate teaching—is another way in which children learn fear. For example, a parent might caution a child against going near the water because it is too dangerous. What she intended was to keep the child from going near the brook or the pond. Instead the child begins to generalize—swimming pools, baths and showers are all water to him. A more common example is the mother who sends the child off to school with the remark "Be careful." What she really intended to tell the child was to wait for the traffic guard to take her across, but instead the child gets the message that danger is all around and thus develops an indiscriminate fear of the outside world. So, when cautioning children about specific things, use specific terms. It is too easy to convey a general fear rather than a specific warning.

Faulty understanding can occur in other ways as well. Two-year-old Mary began to play with the vacuum cleaner. She accidentally started the motor. The noise frightened her, and now she is afraid of all vacuum cleaners—even when the motor is off. Sean, age three, received an inoculation from a doctor wearing a white coat. Sean then developed a fear of anyone dressed in white (the baker and the housepainter) and anyone with the title of Doctor (the psychologist and professor of botany). To a large extent fears of this sort cannot be prevented. It might help to explain that people other than physicians wear white jackets, but connections that are obvious to adults cannot always be grasped by children. Fortunately this kind of fear is usually transitory. A child will soon learn that the baker's product is much more pleasant than the physician's and that professors of botany generally tend to be agreeable characters.

Fears also develop when pleasant consequences follow fear and reinforce it. Let's suppose, for example, that Mary—the girl afraid of the vacuum cleaner—was cuddled by her father right after her fright and given some ice cream. Suppose further that the same sequence happened a second and third time. Pretty soon an association is formed among fright, crying and comfort (probably on an unconscious level). The child might then learn that there is a real payoff to being frightened—at least when Daddy is around.

Fears present parents with a genuine dilemma. Frightened children need to be comforted and reassured, but at the same time you have to be careful that comforting and attention do not reinforce the fear. Fortunately, most of the time young children are pretty obvious when they are feigning hurt and fear, so you can usually tell when they are trying to control you. Sometimes, though, it is not so obvious (when is the child genuinely afraid of the dark and when is he or she trying to prolong the bedtime hour?). You always have to balance the two. Keep in mind this question: Am I being manipulated, even inadvertently, in situations involving fear? It might keep you out of at least a few traps.

Children can learn to cope with fear, and you as a parent can help them do it. Let's take up prevention first, then ways of overcoming fears that already exist.

Preventing Fear

One powerful preventive method is to reinforce risk-taking on the part of a child. Risk-taking will help children develop the kind of personality that can take fear in stride and convert it into something to be overcome rather than a reason not to do something. The following incident shows how risk-taking can be developed or blunted.

David was five. He enjoyed being active. His family took him ice skating and he loved it. After a while he wasn't content just to skate back and forth; he wanted to copy the big boys on the rink who were twirling around and cutting figures. David had their zest but not their skill. He fell, scraped his chin, and bit his lip so hard it began to bleed. His mother took in the situation and said, "Terrific try. You almost did it. That's fantastic. If you hold your arms out to balance yourself while you're going around, I think you'll be able to do it next time." David picked himself up, wiped the blood on his sleeve and tried again. It took him four or five more attempts to master it, but he finally did.

But let's suppose that his mother had raced over and comforted him when she saw the blood. Suppose she had told him that whirling around on the ice was very dangerous, that he was much too little to try it, and then, still comforting him, taken him away from the rink and bought him hot chocolate.

Was David's mother cruel and callous in the first instance? No, she realized that the best way to teach a child to overcome knocks and disappointments is to encourage him to try again, knowing he will gain a little more skill and experience each time. Would David's mother really be helping him in the second instance? Obviously not, for she would be teaching him that he couldn't do something. Which incident is more likely to develop strength and a belief in the self? In the first instance David was taught to apply himself to overcome risks and fear of failure. In the second handling of the incident, David was being taught to accept limitations.

Caution and prudence certainly need to be exercised in encouraging risk-taking (children's judgments are not always sound), yet everyone has to learn to live with risks, and the more practice we get as children the better we can handle them as adults. As a child it is better to suffer disappointment and a few bruised knees than to become afraid to try.

Sports and other physical activities are good areas in which to encourage risk-taking. Rock climbing and skiing are naturals (and reasonably safe, too, if you show your child what to do and then stay beside her while she is learning), as are most sports. Children can also be encouraged to take risks in block building, creative play and games and puzzles. Encourage a child to guess at a riddle or to find out what will happen if he puts one more block on the tower he is building. The child will fail sometimes, but don't we all? When a child gets in the habit of taking risks, the fears that do develop can more readily be overcome.

Overcoming Fear

Reassuring a child and offering verbal explanations of what the child fears are the most obvious ways of dealing with fear. Unfortunately, these are not always effective in and of themselves, because they do not teach a child how to cope directly with the things that frighten him. But they do no harm, and occasionally they may even be sufficient to dispel the fear.

You can reassure a child that monsters do not exist and that thunder does not harm. You can even explain to a child what causes thunder and lightning or shadows or whatever else is bothering her. You don't have to worry too much about your knowledge of physics and science, because the trust the child has in you is more important than the accuracy of the information you give. The important thing is to gear your explanation to the child's level of understanding. It is very easy to talk over a child's head.

It is also important to listen to a child when he expresses fears and not jump right in with an explanation. Try to understand exactly what it is that he fears. It might not be a stranger per se that evokes the fear, but rather the fear that the stranger is a "robber." Similarly, the child might not be afraid of thunder itself, but of the monster in the sky that produces the noise. Only careful listening (and sometimes good guessing) can get at the real source of the fear.

Fear of death is one area in which reassurance is definitely called for. This fear can be divided into two categories—fear that a parent will die and fear of the child's own death.

Let's assume that neither is a realistic fear. (Facing the reality of death is outside the scope of this book, but the work of Dr. Elisabeth Kübler-Ross is recommended for an extensive and sensitive discussion of this topic.) First, try to identify the precise fear—i.e., what is the child really afraid of? Ask her directly and gently what is really bothering her. The child might have a very concrete question and be satisfied with a simple answer. It is important that you neither go beyond the needs of the child nor impose your own fears and fantasies on her. Unless you listen carefully, you may never hear the question.

When a child voices worries about a parent's death, he is often really wondering who will take care of him. Let the child know that the chances of your dying while he or she is very young are infinitely small (if that is true), and that if it should happen, the youngster will always be taken care of. Let him know you have provided for money and a guardian for just such an occasion. Stress that you intend to be around a long time and point out to him how many people are alive who are older than you. If the child asks you what happens when you die, explain simply and straightforwardly what you think, but let him or her know that other people think differently about the subject.

Many children are afraid their parents will get divorced. It's usually best to let a child know where things stand on that matter. If divorce is imminent or possible, assure a child that he or she can cope. First you might want to explain that it is not doing the child much good—or mother and father, either—to live in an atmosphere of tension and fighting. Stress that the child has nothing to do with the decision, that it is something only parents can decide. Many children feel that if they had only behaved better, the divorce would never have happened. Second, point out to him that he has coped before with one parent out of the house. If either parent has ever been on a trip alone, point out how the family managed without the spouse present. Accentuate the positive features of the separation. The parent who is with the child will have more time for the youngster. There will be less fighting and tension. The child can visit the other parent in a different house and see and do different things. Let the child know that other children have parents who are divorced and that they do all right.

Removing the cause of fear will not overcome the fear, but there are still times when it is appropriate to use this method. For example, if a child is simply overwhelmed by fear of the dark, there is nothing wrong with providing a night light. That does not remove the fear, but you can tackle that problem later and more gradually. It is probably best to use this technique sparingly, as children have to learn sooner or later to cope with the things they are afraid of. Removing the problems does little to help children master things. There's nothing more reinforcing than success, so don't deny a child the chance to be successful.

Teaching a child to be knowledgeable about what he fears is the best way to help him overcome fear. Bringing a child into active contact with what is feared—at a pace that is tolerable—is the ideal way to do this. Such contact can come about either in reality or in the child's imagination—it doesn't matter which. The important thing is to have the child gain skill and practice in dealing with what he fears.

The behavioral techniques discussed in previous chapters can help children overcome fears. The three-step method—identify what behavior(s) needs to be increased, reinforce that behavior, and evaluate what you are doing—can be applied to conquering fears in the same way it is used with other problems. Evaluation in this area is not so simple as checking off whether a behavior occurs or doesn't occur, because fear is more elusive than most of the behaviors that have been discussed. Evaluation is likely to be more subjective and even intuitive. But if you observe closely the effect the feared thing has on the child, you should be able to note progress.

Below is a list of ways in which you can teach your child to deal with fear. It makes sense to use a number of these techniques at the same time. And you will have to be patient; fear does not usually disappear overnight, and rushing a child along the path to conquering fear can easily backfire.

1. Provide a model to show the child that he or she won't be hurt by the thing that is feared.
2. Let the child grow accustomed at his or her own speed to what is feared.
3. Introduce by degrees what is feared.
4. Help the child to use his or her imagination to overcome the fear.
5. Teach the child to control what he or she fears.
6. Give the child the skills and understanding to master and understand what he or she fears.

Don't forget to use reinforcement in conjunction with these methods. When the child shows signs of mastering his fear, or even of making attempts to overcome it, reinforce him with encouragement and praise. You can also give him a more tangible reward. For example, if a child who was afraid to go down a small hill on skis accomplishes that feat, let him know how proud you are of him, and follow up the congratulations with a cup of hot chocolate. But the strongest reinforcer for the child will be his own sense of competence and self-confidence.

Now let's see how these techniques can be used.

Providing a Model

Letting a child learn that the feared object will not hurt her is crucial to overcoming fear. Sometimes you have to engineer situations so she will discover this. For example, if she is afraid of the police, you might—in full view of the child—stop a policeman and ask for directions. She will see that the contact did not hurt or frighten you. If she is afraid of dogs, it might be helpful to pat a dog on the head in the youngster's presence and begin to play with the animal. Try to include her in the conversation with the policeman or the play with the dog, for then she will be able to see that no harm will befall her either.

Unfortunately, this method does not always work. Children sometimes retain their fear of animals or police even though parents and other important people set examples of fearlessness. It may be that your fearlessness seems to them unattainable. But even if this method doesn't work right away, there is no harm in continuing to use it. Sometimes it just takes a while for the message to sink in. It is a very big leap for a child to realize that if a thunderstorm won't harm you, it won't harm him or her either. You can add to your effectiveness by letting a child know how frightened you used to be of thunderstorms or merry-go-rounds and the kind of strategy you used as a child to overcome your fear.

Other children often make better models for children than adults do. That is because a child can identify much better with another child than with an adult. Children who are a little bit frightened themselves but manage to overcome the fear are the best models. Brothers or sisters or a child's close friends can often serve this purpose.

If you are using other children as examples, tell your child to watch what Billy and Mary do in a situation. Break down some of the behaviors they engage in. For example, if your child is watching another child climb a tree, point out which limbs are used or how the youngster tests the strength of a limb. At the same time, be quite careful of the words and tone you use. A child can easily interpret the statement, "Why can't you be more like Billy and Mary? They're not afraid to go down the sliding pond," as a put-down and an unfair comparison. The frightened child will usually end up resenting Billy and Mary as well as you, and it will not help solve the problem.

Sometimes children spontaneously use other children as models. For example, Johnny, age four, recoiled with fear when his older sister came home with a Halloween mask. He crawled into his father's lap. His father didn't say a word but just let Johnny observe the other children exchange masks and try on different ones.

Johnny's curiosity and his desire to play with the bigger boys and girls served to overcome the fear. He ended up asking his sister if he could look at the mask up close. Then he asked her to hold it up near him and finally to put it on him. After a while he joined in the games. Fear of masks was never a problem again.

You can even have one child learn from another how to cope with the doctor, dentist and other professionals. Try to arrange for the child to accompany an older child on his visit. It could be a brother or sister or a neighbor's or friend's child. If possible, get one child to be the explicit teacher of the other. (Make sure that the child has been to the dentist or whatever before, and that the visit is for some innocuous purpose like having one's teeth cleaned.) Let the more fearful child watch the other and learn what a visit entails. Most doctors and dentists will cooperate with this kind of program.

A dental association has in fact recently produced a film, *The Red Toothbrush,* in which this approach is demonstrated. In the film a fearful and a fearless child go to the dentist together, and the fearful child watches the dentist clean his friend's teeth. During the course of the film the child learns how the brush operates, how the chair goes up and down, how to get a drink of water, and everything else he might wonder about concerning dentists. Then the child climbs into the chair and has his teeth cleaned.

If you can't arrange to have an introductory trip, read a story to your child about a visit to the dentist, or—better yet—make up a story with a happy ending. There is also nothing wrong with letting your child bring along to the dentist's office a teddy bear or a favorite blanket or whatever else comforts him.

A visit to the dentist is, of course, an excellent occasion to reward a child for not giving in to his fear. In the film mentioned above, the fearless and the fearful child each receive a reward when the work is done. So you might consider scheduling a shopping trip for the sneakers your child wants right after the visit to the dentist.

Letting the Child Grow Accustomed at His or Her Own Speed to What Is Feared

Another effective method of helping a child overcome fear is to deliberately expose him to the feared object. Then allow him to approach it or not, as he wishes. For example, David was afraid of the ocean. He would not go near it, no matter how much his parents urged him. Attempts to lure him into the water failed. His parents finally decided to leave him alone.

David got bored sitting on the beach. Of his own volition he went near the water and let it lap at his toes. His parents said nothing. The next day he began to build sand castles and filled his bucket several times with water. Within a week he had begun to play and splash in the water. Within two weeks he was attempting to teach himself to swim.

Another example: Marilyn was afraid of dogs. Her father brought a friendly dog and tied it up in the back yard. Marilyn was free to approach the dog or not; the decision was entirely hers. It was only a few days before she began to pat the dog. Within a week she asked if it could be untied so they could play together.

Another child was afraid of insects. His parents bought an ant colony—enclosed in glass—and left it lying in the family room. Within a day or two the child began to observe the ant colony. He soon picked it up to get a better look at it. He showed no evidence of fear after that.

This system works even better when a reinforcer is a natural consequence of overcoming fear. Rebecca, age five, was afraid of physically deformed people. The assistant teacher in her kindergarten limped because of polio, and Rebecca shunned her.

When the teacher realized what was happening, she had the assistant give out the toys before recess. Rebecca wanted to play jump rope, and the only way she could get the rope was to go up to the aide. As usual, she balked. The teacher and the assistant said nothing to Rebecca for two days, at which point Rebecca did manage to ask for the jump rope. Within three or four days, Rebecca had lost her fear of the woman, and later she lost her fear of handicapped people in general.

Introducing by Degrees What Is Feared

Susie was frightened by the flow of water from the faucet. To combat her fear, her father adjusted the water so it would flow feebly from the faucet. Susie soon got accustomed to the thin stream of water. Over a period of days, her father gradually allowed the water to flow more freely. Finally, Susie could tolerate (more accurately, she didn't even notice) water flowing out of the tap at full force.

Other instances of this method: Johnny, four years old, was beginning to look like a sheep dog. The first time he was taken to a barber shop he became so frightened he had a tantrum and simply refused to let the barber cut his hair. His father took him home. He still needed the haircut, so his mother decided to take him back on a day when it wasn't so crowded. She told Johnny she knew the situation frightened him terribly, and she was sorry about that. Still, she assured him, there was no need to worry—she would cut his hair. Johnny climbed onto the chair, and his mother, with the aid of the barber, put the bib over him and began to cut his hair. When he was safely acclimated to the chair, the bib and the cutting, she stepped back, telling Johnny that the barber was more skilled than she was at cutting hair and that she was going to let him finish the job. The barber took over while Johnny's mother stood near him. The next time Johnny had to have his hair cut, he did not put up a fuss.

Getting the child accustomed by degrees to what is feared takes ingenuity, but it works. You can also use reinforcers effectively by rewarding his progress at every stage.

Sally was afraid of horses and cows. At the sight of them she would scream and try to hide. For most children this wouldn't have been a big problem, but Sally lived in farm country; sometimes she had to go through a pasture to get to a friend's or neighbor's house.

Her mother read Sally some stories about horses and looked at pictures of them with her. When Sally was able to tolerate looking at the pictures, her mother brought out toy animals and they "played farm" together.

Then, when her mother felt she was ready, she took Sally to a corral gate. The mother rewarded Sally with a token. Her mother told her that when she had earned four tokens she could have a ride on the tractor-mower, which she had always wanted to ride. They waited awhile at the gate and then walked into the corral. As soon as Sally passed the gate, her mother gave her another token. They then walked to the barn door. She was again rewarded, and she received still another token just for looking at the animals in their stalls. Then they went home, and Sally was able to turn in her tokens for a ride.

The following day Sally and her mother went directly to the barn door. The mother gave Sally a token. When they entered the barn she was given another one, and then one for every five feet that they walked into the barn. Sally was given three tokens for touching the horse's muzzle. By the end of the day she had lost most of her fear of horses, and had earned another tractor-mower ride as well.

Using Imagination to Overcome Fears

Children's fears of things that exist only in their imagination (ghosts, bogeymen and so forth) are quite commonplace. Fears of this kind are harder to overcome than fears of real things such as animals or vacuum cleaners, and more debilitating as well, because there are no opportunities to confront objects of these fears. Nonetheless, children have to learn to deal with them, and the best way to accomplish this is for you to enlist your child's imagination in dealing with her fear.

Manuel, age four, had invented a fearsome dog, with a shape somewhere between that of a dinosaur and that of a wolf. It could destroy people and houses in a matter of seconds. But the dog got out of hand and began to scare him too. It sometimes kept him up at night and prevented him from napping in the afternoon. Even during active play there were occasions when Manuel became frightened of the monster.

His mother talked to Manuel about the imaginary creature. First she tried to reassure him that no such thing existed and suggested he forget about it. She also promised him that she and his father would always protect him. But the fear didn't disappear; if anything, it got worse.

Working on the theory that if you can't lick them, join them, Manuel's mother entered into his imaginary play. She brought the monster into the play too and began to wrestle with it. She and Manuel put a magic collar around the monster's neck and tamed it. It became Manuel's pet and eventually his protector.

May, age four, was terrified because a robber lurked under her bed at night. Moving the bed and showing her that nothing was there did not help. Her father gave her a flashlight. Together in play they transformed it into a magic ray gun. May was told that in an emergency she could turn on the flashlight and shine it at the robber, and he would disintegrate. She liked that word. The first night she played with the flashlight a lot, and even went to sleep with it on. She slept through the night without crying out in terror. In a few days she had convinced herself that her magic ray gun had done away with the robber. She lost her fear of being alone in the room and her fear of robbers.

This same technique worked with a six-year-old boy who was afraid to fall asleep because of bad dreams concerning spiders. His mother and the boy concocted a special spider repellent made of flour and water and vegetable dye and placed some pellets of it around the bed. He had little trouble falling asleep after that.

You can often suggest to children that they imagine Wonder Woman or Batman and Robin accompanying them on their tasks. Who wouldn't feel safer walking into a dark closet with Wonder Woman at her side? With such allies many a child has overcome his or her fear of a dark hallway or a dimly lit cellar. You can also have children imagine they are Wonder Woman or Batman when they are in fearful situations.

You can also help a child overcome fears of imaginary creatures by *gently* bringing the child into contact with the place where the creature abides. For example, Anita was afraid to go into closets. She and her mother sometimes had tea parties. One day her mother set up the tea party just outside a closet that Anita feared. Anita joined in the game even though the closet door was open. The mother and Anita put the dolls' coats in the closet and went in there several times during the course of the party. Through actively getting the child to play near and in the closet, the mother helped her daughter overcome her fear of closets.

Children often have fears of cellars and closets, closed trunks and boxes, hallways that are dark, and other places where evil forces might lurk. They will gradually lose their fears if they enter and explore these places as part of their actual experiences. For example, you might organize an Easter egg hunt and place the eggs just inside a darkened hallway (of course, the eggs have to be at least partially visible) or in some other judicious place. This built-in reinforcer will motivate children to peek into the feared boxes or pass through the hall.

In a variant of this technique, a psychologist directed a teenage boy with an intense fear of dogs to imagine himself a driver of a sleek sports car that had just won an important race. The boy was to imagine driving around town with throngs of people coming out to greet him. Then a small dog was to come over to the car and sniff around. The child imagined the same scene over and over again, erasing the image from his mind when it became too vivid, until he felt no anxiety about the dog. Ultimately the child lost his fear of dogs.

You can ask older children to imagine going through things they fear in their own minds. Fourteen-year-old Mark was a very conscientious student. For one reason or another he hadn't very thoroughly practiced a piece that the band was to play. He developed stomach cramps and didn't want to go to school.

Mark's father asked him to imagine the scene that would have to take place sooner or later with his teacher. He advised Mark to imagine one element at a time. When that element became too vivid, he was to erase the scene from his mind. Mark was to imagine, for example, getting up that day, walking to school, getting through attendance and so forth. Only when he was comfortable with that sequence was Mark to imagine meeting the teacher. Finally Mark imagined the teacher reprimanding him. After going through the scene several times in his mind, Mark found that although he didn't like the reprimand, he could face up to it.

Controlling What Is Feared

Almost everyone is afraid of the unknown, and just think how much there is that little children don't yet know. To a little child a radio can be a monstrous creation that barks out strange noises. If a child is afraid of a radio or phonograph, you can reduce this fear by showing him or her how to control it by pushing the on-off button. Do the same with fans and other appliances that work by electricity. One little girl was afraid of falling off things. When her father taught her how to climb, she lost her fear. If a child is afraid of wind-up toys that move around, teach the child how they work and draw her into play with them. Let her wind up the toy herself. If a child is afraid of shadows, create a few by cupping your hands into different positions, and show your child how to do the same. The more you teach a child how to control things—dishwashers, locks, even fires—the more readily he or she will overcome any fear of these things.

Teaching a child to control animals can be particularly helpful in reducing fear of them. For example, Arlene, age thirteen, was afraid of dogs. She was particularly afraid of a St. Bernard that lived near her. Arlene sometimes walked blocks out of her way to avoid contact with the dog. One day her mother showed Arlene how to shoo the dog away and make him go home. She lost her fear not only of that particular dog but of dogs in general.

Gaining Techniques to Master and Understand What Is Feared

Often children are afraid of other children. For example, Billy, age seven, refused to go outside to play. His parent discovered he was afraid of a bully in the neighborhood. His mother, a judo enthusiast, decided to teach Billy some rudimentary fighting skills and ways to deal with teasing. She showed him a few judo holds. In addition, they did a lot of role-playing and rehearsed a potential confrontation between the bully and Billy. The mother had her son act the part of the bully. The mother modeled how to stand up to the bully and how to ignore or return insults as the situation warranted. She taught him when to raise his voice and when to lower it, when to stare the other person in the eye and when to avoid eye contact. She also pointed out when to fight if necessary. They acted out several possible incidents and went over the situations repeatedly. The boy was finally able to go out and deal with the bully.

Role-playing can be an invaluable tool in teaching children the skills and confidence they need to overcome fearful situations. It gives a child practice in a safe and comfortable place and can be used with children of any age. It is especially good for handling problems outside the home.

Mary, age ten, had a teacher who picked on her. Every time she answered a question, the teacher replied with a wisecrack. The time came when Mary was afraid to answer a question. When her father discovered that Mary wasn't provoking the situation, he sat down with her and discussed strategies for handling the problem. They decided that a private conversation in which Mary would share her discomfort with the teacher would be the first thing to try.

Her father made believe he was the teacher. He instructed Mary to set up an appointment with him. At first she did not look him in the eye, and she asked for the appointment in such a small voice that he couldn't hear her. He praised her effort, then showed her how to look at him directly and ask for the appointment in a stronger voice. She tried it and succeeded. Then she was at a loss for what to say. He had her play the part of the teacher, and he played her part. "She" (the father) voiced her discomfort at the ridicule and explained why it made her so uncomfortable. "She" asked what she was doing wrong and what would have to be done to rectify the situation. They took turns playing each role and gave each other feedback as to how they were doing in their respective roles.

Finally, in reality, Mary was able to let her teacher know how she felt about the problem. It turned out to be a situation that was easily changed. The teacher said he hadn't realized he was being so sarcastic, but now that he knew, he would watch out for it. He said he would appreciate Mary's letting him know when he acted sarcastic. He ended up thanking Mary for initiating the conversation.

Athletics is another area that can evoke a lot of fears in children. Many children are afraid they don't measure up to a standard and so will not try. In school they are afraid they won't be chosen for a team. Practice playing catch or kickball with a child if you can. Get another child or the babysitter to help if possible. Teach him to say "I blew it," if appropriate, and then continue with the game. Work with the teacher if possible so the child can at least learn the rules of the game before playing. At the same time, you should be sure the teacher has worked out a reasonable schedule: every child, regardless of talent, should have the right to participate in sports. You can also use role-playing to teach your child where and how to stand when players are being chosen, what to say, how to shout encouragement to teammates, and any other behavior the child needs to play the game.

You can reinforce children with a material reward when they have learned how to play a game or master a situation, but generally the reward of accomplishment will be enough. Success is the most gratifying reinforcer of all.

Combining the Techniques

As mentioned before, a combination of the above techniques can also be effective in certain situations. The fear of being alone is a good example of such a situation.

Many children are afraid to be alone, either in their own rooms when other people are in the house or in the house when the parents go out. First find out, if you can, why the child is afraid. It may be that he is afraid of a "robber" or of a ghost. If so, you can use the techniques described in the section on imaginary fears. You might also suggest that the child switch on the TV or begin to read or work on a project if the fears persist. If he is occupied, he is much less likely to become frightened.

The first few times children are left alone in the house they will be afraid. After all, it is a new experience for them. You can help make this kind of fear less intense by observing the following guidelines.

1. Let the child get used to being alone in the daytime.
2. Leave explicit instructions as to where you can be reached in an emergency. Also discuss explicitly what should be done in emergencies. Let the child know that help is always available.
3. Make staying alone an honor. Give the child extra privileges to go with that honor so she feels there is a real payoff to being mature and staying home alone. Initially, some parents even pay their children the money that would have gone to the babysitter.
4. Leave the child alone for gradually increasing lengths of time. At first just stay out of the house for thirty minutes. When that is tolerable to the child, stay away for an hour; keep on increasing the time until she is used to being alone for the evening.

Professional Consultation

If your child has a great many fears that are causing him or her misery, there is nothing wrong with contacting a psychologist or psychiatrist. Those with behavioral backgrounds are particularly skilled in removing fears. Fears of real objects can usually be overcome quite quickly. Fears of imaginary objects are considerably more difficult but can still be dealt with. But first try to change things yourself.

What Not to Do

You have little to gain and a lot to lose by forcing a child into contact with things he fears. Forced contact usually strengthens fear. For every child who has learned how to swim by being forced into the water, there are a hundred who learned to fear the water more intensely. For every child who was ridiculed and shamed into playing football when he was afraid of being hurt or making a fool of himself, there are a hundred whose fears have been confirmed and who are convinced that football is to be shunned. Forced contact only makes fear that much harder to conquer.

Making a child feel cowardly or inadequate is also something to be avoided. It is much better to let a child know that everyone is afraid of something, and that you know that when he is ready he will conquer his fear. Children generally live up to their parents' expectations, and conquering fear is no different from other behaviors in this regard.

Ignoring fears is also ineffective. Many parents make it a policy to deliberately ignore a child's fears or to distract her when she asks questions about something she fears, such as divorce or an operation. Ignoring is a good policy to follow if the child is trying to get adult attention by simulating a fear, or even to control adults with his "fears"—e.g., the child who feigns fright of the cellar to avoid doing an errand or the child who pretends to be afraid of the dark in order to get his bedtime postponed. But in general ignoring is not an effective, or humane, technique for removing or mitigating real fears. Many fears diminish in time because of increased age and experience and understanding, but if your child is really afraid of something, you have to actively meet the situation. Loving is caring, and caring means doing something about a problem. There is no payoff in the long run for pretending that a problem doesn't exist.

CHAPTER IX

Schools

School is important. Next to the bedroom, where the majority of time is spent in sleep, a child spends more time in a schoolroom than in any other single place. By the time a child reaches junior high school, he or she will have spent more than 7,000 hours in classrooms. And this is excluding nursery school. Teachers see more of a child than the average father and many mothers. The school experience, for better or worse, has a deep effect on a child's happiness and well-being. It also affects his adult life, because self-concept, attitudes toward learning and authority, and basic skills are at least partially formed during school years.

It pays to get children off to a good start. Schools demand three different kinds of skills—self-help, intellectual, and self-control—that are sufficiently developed so that a child will behave and can learn in a setting consisting of a number of children and only one adult.

The self-help skills include self-toileting (including zipping up flies or pulling down panties), knowing how and when to blow one's nose, pouring one's own milk, eating without help, getting into and out of outer garments, tying shoes, and generally taking care of oneself so that an undue burden is not placed on the teacher. If you employ the three-step method, you should have little trouble teaching the necessary skills.

Most of the intellectual skills a child needs for school (vocabulary, concepts, following instructions, answering questions) are implicit in the parents' training. You can teach these skills even better if you are conscious of what you are doing. Let's begin by examining how these basic skills can be taught.*

Reading to your child and making trips to the library stimulate general intellectual development. Singing and listening to records teach a child to focus attention and to enjoy music. Trips to the zoo, museum and different stores broaden your child's knowledge. Often libraries show nature movies and present puppet shows that are especially geared to young children.

Having young children participate in play groups and nursery school prepares them both intellectually and socially for kindergarten.

Intellectual Preparation

Vocabulary

Most vocabulary is learned by imitation. If you wanted to teach a child the names of the utensils, you might proceed this way: "This is a spoon. What is it?" Let the child say the right word. If she has trouble, let her say it with you. When the right response comes out, reinforce it with exclamations of delight. "That's correct, Melissa. That's fantastic." And then go on: "This is a fork, Melissa. What is it?" and so on through any words you think important for her to know. When you use this method, phase out your cues gradually.

Teaching should not be a dull intellectual exercise. Learning should always be fun for a child. While she's still in the crib, you can play with her toes and say, "This is a toe. What is this?" and so on through her fingers, ears, nose, eyes, belly button, knees, vagina, and everything else. A kiss and a hug are usually an ample reward.

Once you've taught a youngster basic vocabulary, motivate her to use it. Don't respond to grunts and pointing, even though you know perfectly well what she means. Insist on words. When she can use complete sentences, don't settle for anything less. If she wants her blanket and just points at it, don't respond. Have her say, "I want my blanket"

* A very helpful and explicit book on the subject is called *Give Your Child a Superior Mind* by Siegfried and Therese Engelmann (New York, Simon & Schuster, 1966).

(using whatever name she uses), before you hand her the blanket. Similarly, have the child say, "Please pass the bread," before you give it to her.

Concepts

Most concepts can be taught quite naturally. For example, consider "up and down." Children like to be picked up, but sometimes they will say, "Pick me down." Teach the child the correct phrase. Have her imitate you. *When* she says it correctly, *then* pick her up. Do not pick her up when she says, "Pick me down." After a while she will learn to differentiate between the two words.

Make a game out of teaching concepts. Let's take "in and out" as an example. Have the child learn one of these words at a time. First, put a ball in a box and say, "I am putting the ball in the box. What am I doing?" When the child can say, "You are putting the ball in the box" (or drawer or pocket), then take the ball out of the box or drawer and say, "I am taking the ball out of the box" (or whatever other container you are using). "What am I doing?" When she has mastered *out* as well as *in,* then do the two words closer together. Practice (play is really a more accurate word) until the child can correctly say whether the ball is going out of the box or into the box. Give your approval and praise for every correct answer, and throw in a raisin occasionally for fun.

Following Instructions

The ability to follow instructions is another important prerequisite for school. By the time a child is two he or she should be capable of following a host of instructions: brush your teeth, take a cookie from the cookie jar, wait here for a minute while I run back into the house. Such training will stand the child in good stead in school. If he cannot follow directions by age three, it's time to work on that directly. If you use rewards and a game format, you'll have little trouble teaching that kind of skill. For example, "I bought you a little present today" (some soldiers or bubble bath). "If you look in the bottom drawer of the kitchen cabinet you'll find it" will capture almost any child's ear and provide him or her with the motivation to follow directions.

Answering Questions

The ability to ask and answer questions is also an important prerequisite for school. Liven up your meals by asking riddles. Start with very easy ones at first: "Who is wearing a red shirt today? Are the noodles hot or cold? Name three things we eat with." These usually get a good response from children. Then, when your child has the hang of it, have her ask you a question. Make it into a game. Have her stump you once in a while. If your child knows any arithmetic facts or the names of any baseball teams, make up a contest. Children love contests, especially if they sometimes win.

Social Preparation

If you anticipate that your child will have difficulty in school, you may want to alert the teacher to the way he or she behaves. If the teacher knows what your child is like, he or she will not be so likely to require the child to do something he cannot do at that time.

It's usually a good idea to visit his future classroom anyway. The atmosphere and the way the children dress and behave are important to know about. If everyone comes to school in blue jeans, you probably won't want to dress your child in a suit; if sneakers are standard footwear in a community, your child will feel odd in dress shoes. This does not mean that you and your child have to be slavish devotees to whatever fad comes along. But school is a hard enough adjustment to make anyhow, so why complicate it at the beginning by making your child look different?

It's also helpful to become acquainted with the teacher before problems arise; you can then work together more easily. Also, if you know what the school requirements are, you can go over the rules beforehand with a child. Don't do this in a threatening way. Just let him know how things are done in school. For example, your child should know that Mrs. Jones doesn't want children to talk during a class lesson and that you expect him to obey the teacher. If he knows that you and the teacher are united, he is much more likely to be obedient.

As a general rule, children should go off to school on their own, figuratively if not literally. It is noteworthy that on the first day of school in rural areas there are far fewer children weeping in the halls for their parents than there are in urban areas, the reason being that in the country, the children are taken off to school by bus, and there is not much mileage to be gained by crying for a mother or father who is twenty miles away. If you take your child to school, leave him or her there and let the teacher take over. If it is necessary to stay in the classroom with her, pay as little attention to her as possible. Read a book instead.

Dealing with Problems at School

Lack of Readiness

What should a parent do when a teacher finds a child difficult to handle and even questions whether he or she is ready for first grade? Find out specifically what the child does or does not do that is causing the difficulty. A home-school reinforcement system can rectify most problems if the goals are clear enough and everyone is consistent.

David was a very young five when he entered kindergarten. He was the last of six children, and his mother wanted desperately to leave domesticity and go to work. At the April conference Mrs. Fuscoe was informed that David was having a lot of trouble settling down and that he lacked the skills and the maturity necessary for first grade.

Mrs. Fuscoe was heartbroken. She seriously doubted she could get through another year at home, but she didn't want to go to work until all the children were in school for a full day. She decided that David was going to learn to be mature and to master the skills necessary to get along in first grade no matter what. She asked the teacher to write out a specific list of skills that David needed for first grade. The list reads as follows:

1. Print his first and last names.
2. Be able to read his first and last names.
3. Tell the name of each letter.
4. Know the alphabet by heart.
5. Write each letter.
6. Tell the sound of each letter.
7. Tell which words start with the same sound. For example, ball and bat are the same; glove and happy are different.
8. Count up to 20.

9. Be able to tell what number comes before and after a given number. For example, 17—16 comes before, and 18 comes after.

Mrs. Fuscoe also asked David's teacher to send home a note each day commenting on David's conduct in school.

Mrs. Fuscoe then took David to the shoe store to buy him the speedy sneakers he had coveted for so long. She also bought the toy machine gun he had asked for and some bubble-gum baseball cards. She figured that the fifteen dollars it cost her was very little compared to the value of her mental health.

She made a deal with David. The sneakers were for big boys. He was allowed to wear them only when his teacher sent home a favorable note. If the note was not good, off would go the sneakers and he would have to wear his hiking boots instead. When he received ten good notes he would receive the machine gun, no strings attached. Up went the following chart on the refrigerator door:

M	T	W	Th	F
X	X			

Each time the teacher sent home a good note, a big red X was placed in one of the squares.

Each afternoon Mrs. Fuscoe worked with David on his academic skills. She explained their importance to David. Their work had to be completed before he was allowed to watch any TV shows. The reinforcers used were baseball cards, along with praise and hugs. Exceptionally good work was rewarded with the bubble gum that accompanied the card. She and David also practiced these skills in the car whenever they went shopping or had to run errands.

It took Mrs. Fuscoe a lot of afternoons to teach David the skills he needed to know. She made it into a routine, but she tried to make it as much fun as possible. To that end they made up a lot of games and contests. She kept a list, and every time David learned another skill, they both celebrated. When September came around, Mrs. Fuscoe went to work, and David entered first grade.

Actually this kind of problem should have been solved much earlier in the year. A parent should make her concern explicit to the teacher: "If there are any problems, please let me know right away. If I can help, I will." Every teacher in every grade should be told that. Parent/teacher conferences should be as specific as Mrs. Fuscoe's. The practice of having a teacher write down the exact skills that need to be learned is a good one that can be used in all grades.

Underachieving and Poor Grades

Don't panic if your child brings home poor grades. You're not perfect; your child's not perfect. Nor is the teacher perfect. You don't always do your best, and neither does anyone else. Visit the classroom once or twice to get a better perspective on what's happening. Speak privately with the teacher to find out what you can do to help the situation. Also let him or her know your child's good points. Some teachers need to be told that.

Think about what the teacher says. She is not always right, nor does she always see what she is doing to contribute to the problem. At the same time, be sure you have a positive attitude toward her, and find something good to say about her work with your child.

There's no point in dwelling on poor grades or on what the child is not doing. That only reinforces that behavior. Keep on telling the child what he or she is doing right. Tell him why you think he should do at least reasonably well in school.

Consider whether your goal should necessarily be the improvement of grades. It might be that the child is doing all he or she can at the moment and has to work on consolidating earlier skills. Keeping a child's enthusiasm alive will do more for the child than pushing for straight A's.

Recognize that there are different kinds of underachievers. One problem might be that the child is preoccupied with making friends or socializing. That is quite common in teenagers, but it happens earlier too. Again, you have to weigh the two needs and decide which is more important. Sometimes it is more important for the child to have friends than to make high grades, and sometimes you have to help the child cut down on his or her social life until school receives its due. Your decision should depend on the circumstances.

Some children have one or two deep interests, and academics—at least the way the school presents them—are not high priorities. Behavior programs are very effective with this kind of underachieving, since the reinforcement is so apparent. Receiving a book on geology or new paintbrushes can be made contingent on improving school performance.

Two other kinds of underachievers would be the very shy child who is too timid to speak up in class, and the overactive child. Refer to the next chapter for a discussion of how you can help these children adapt to their social surroundings.

If you point the child's problems out to the teacher, he or she may make future demands more realistic. You might want to role-play some situations with a shy child. Have the youngster practice saying the answer out loud with you, and let him or her know by deed as well as word that mistakes are not tragic.

If you have a very active child, encourage the teacher to be realistic about what he can do now and ask that some of his work be sent home each day so that you can help the youngster learn the skills. Also, encourage the teacher to give the child short assignments that can be completed easily. Giving an active child monitor jobs contingent on completing tasks can serve a double purpose. The job can both act as a reinforcer for completing the task and allow the child to discharge energy constructively.

A warning about underachievement: don't be a pushy parent. You may end up with a dawdler who is afraid of pressure.

Resistance to School

What should you do if your child resists going to school? Getting off to school is hard for some children. They may cry or even vomit. Some children, in fact, control their parents by vomiting in the morning. The rituals of changing and commiseration that result help neither the parent nor the child. Try to find out whether anything is going on at school that is troubling the child—a bully or a lunchroom situation, for example, or a teacher who is always hollering at the child. Try to correct the situation, and let your child know exactly what has been done to remedy things. Let him know you're on his side and will do everything you can to help, but he must understand that school attendance is not optional. Nor are you available to take him home if he gets sick. It's important to take a hard line on that matter. You don't want a child to learn that he can avoid unpleasant situations by getting sick or upset.

Send the child off to school with a very light breakfast—or no breakfast at all—to reduce the nausea problem. Do not get into long discussions with her about school or about her not feeling well. Many children with a fear of school would like nothing better than to discuss their problems all day long. Let the parent who is firmer with discipline take the child to school in a very matter-of-fact manner. Discuss baseball, the weather and politics with the child, but not school. When you get there, drop the child off and leave right away.

A program should be planned with the guidance counselor and the teacher. Everyone should work together to see how the problem may be solved. Reducing expectations might be the answer.

Sometimes the teacher will have to excuse the child a number of times to go to the bathroom—a direct indication of how nervous the child is. Many children will throw up in school too. It has been found that if the child is merely given a sponge to clean up things while the teacher goes on with the lesson, vomiting decreases rather quickly. Again, that is something the school should handle.

When the child returns home from school, compliment him for sticking it out, no matter how many times he got sick or how miserable an experience he had. You and the child can be proud of his just staying there, as it was undoubtedly difficult for him. You are likely to have the same sort of difficulty the next few days, but it will become less serious. When the child comes home from school each day, compliment him for doing so much better. Stress the fact that he is overcoming his fears.

Usually after a few days the complaining, stomach upsets and so forth will have diminished considerably. That is the time to throw a small party for your child and let him know how proud you are of him. You can also tie a reward to school attendance.

If this kind of program does not work after a few weeks, discussion with a mental health professional might well be in order.

Homework Problems

Homework is a good indicator of what's happening with your child at school. A first grader who comes home from school and makes believe he has homework is telling you he enjoys learning and acting like an older child. A child who comes home cursing about his assignment is also telling you something. The child who fails to bring home any assignments, even though you know his classmates have homework, is telling you something so important you can't neglect it. But first let's talk about homework in general.

Consider saving returned homework papers and other papers. It's always helpful, especially in the lower grades, to bring them out after a few months so your child can see the progress he's made in punctuation and in the way he writes his name, and the kind of problems he used to struggle over. That can give a child a real feeling of achievement. Having a bulletin board where you can hang up papers is also a good idea. Keep a mental note of progress, and praise improvement.

Johnny Smith was in second grade and could barely read beginning first grade material. Nevertheless, he had an air of self-confidence that was unusual for a second-grader. His teacher remarked to his mother and asked her what she did to bring it out. Mrs. Smith replied: "I always look at his papers with him and show him how much better he's getting when he does do better. I show him how many more words he spells correctly each week and how many fewer errors he makes. He knows he's improving, so why shouldn't he feel good? He's come a long, long way."

A child should be reasonably clear about his assignments and what he is expected to do. It might help to get him a small pad on which to jot down the assignments and to go over with him how he can best use it. Attach importance to the pad by telling him how grown up he is now that he can use one. You can also ask to see the pad on occasion, so he'll know you think it's important and worth discussing with him.

A parent can help a child a great deal by establishing homework routines. It usually pays to make sure the homework is done before the TV goes on. You might set up a system in which the child does his or her work from four-thirty to five-thirty each day, or right after the dinner dishes have been washed. In the lower grades especially you should consider a routine in which you discuss the assignment with the child after it has been completed. Don't fall into the trap, though, of doing all his work for him. It is sometimes better to let a child work out difficulties with his teacher without your intervention, so you have to use judgment here.

A child should be able to complete a homework assignment fairly readily. If your child consistently has difficulty with homework, a conference with the teacher is very much in order. Try to find out why he is having the difficulty. Perhaps he doesn't know how to study. If so, you might try teaching him the SQRRR method:

S—The student first *surveys* the material he was assigned in order to find out the general content.

Q—The next step is to set up *questions.* If the material itself does not contain questions at the end of the chapter, teach the youngster to convert topic headings into questions. For example, if the topic headings are "Housing of Eskimos" and "Recreational Activities of Eskimos," have the child change these into "What kind of housing do Eskimos have?" and "What are the recreational activities of Eskimos?"

R—The next step is for the child to *read* the material with a view to answering the questions that were posed in the previous step. The child should be instructed to read with special care those paragraphs and sentences that contain answers to the questions.

R—*Review* comes next. Have the child turn away from the book and answer the questions aloud. If he can answer the questions, go on to the next step. If he can't answer the questions, he will have to reread the material and study it until he can.

R—*Recite.* At the end of the chapter, the child should take a break. When he comes back, he should try to answer all the questions again. If he doesn't succeed, let him go over the material again. If he can answer the questions, you can assume he has learned the material.

If the child is still unable to do the work, you may have to teach him yourself. Ask the teacher to be specific about what has to be learned and have him or her give you the materials to work with.

Number facts and reading vocabulary can be taught by a parent. Make up a set of flash cards with numbers or words on them. The teacher will show you how to do this if you don't know how. Time the child as he goes through the cards. Bet him a dime he can't do it any faster next time around. Help him keep a graph of the progress he's making. When he finds he's getting better in school, he will begin to work that much harder.

If a child gets stuck on a homework problem or is having a difficult time doing his work, encourage her to take a little break or a few deep breaths and then try again. When you're teaching, avoid words and phrases like "Think" and "You could do it if you really wanted to." Instead, say something like "I like that approach," or "Can you figure out another way of handling that?" Avoid making comparisons between the child and a brother or sister or anyone else. Belittling helps no one. Praise the child for trying even when the answers are not correct. Children's feelings get hurt very easily when it comes to school work, and being made to feel inadequate can have a terrible effect on their self-concept.

The following case study shows how a parent can help a child in school. Tommy Ryan, age nine, was reading more than one grade behind his class. He was a good student in all his other subjects. A thorough physical examination showed nothing wrong. His teacher felt that one of Tommy's difficulties was that he was so frightened of failing that he wouldn't even try. His parents decided to try teaching him themselves. His teacher gave them a set of self-correcting reading texts which they used to work with him at home.

1. *Identify the behavior to be increased or decreased.* Mrs. Ryan and Tommy took turns reading pages from a second-grade reader. It took Tommy three minutes to read one page aloud. He made mistakes on six of every ten words. When he had finished reading the page, he couldn't remember what he had read.

Mrs. Ryan could not determine precisely why Tommy was reading so poorly. The only thing she could figure out was that his poor reading got him some adult attention, and that for him avoiding reading was more comfortable than trying to read, for when he tried to read he felt inadequate and even stupid.

Based on what the teacher had said and on their own experiences with Tommy, Ryans decided to increase his rate of reading, the number of words he could read correctly and his ability to understand what he was reading.

2. *Intervene.* Mrs. Ryan set up a specific time and place to teach Tommy. Thirty-minute lessons were scheduled each day. No one was allowed to interrupt during this period. Mrs. Ryan set up a reinforcement program: *when* Tommy successfully completed a page, *then* he could earn one point toward a prize of his choice. She explicitly communicated what successful completion meant—answering correctly four out of five questions about the material he had read, and making fewer than one error for every eight words.

The materials, which were programmed, lent themselves to short work sessions and to the teaching of specific skills. Even though Mrs. Ryan was not a trained teacher, she could follow the teacher's manual with little trouble. She realized that if she asked too much of Tommy too soon, failure would result, so she made sure she started out a little bit below his level. As Tommy became more comfortable with the materials, the teaching sessions grew longer. She kept the lessons as simple and as positive as she could. Each session was followed by a game.

Whenever Tommy mastered a new skill, it was met with bursts of praise and encouraging comments and entered on a list. He began to take great pride in this list, especially when it grew longer and longer. He also began to take great pride in the number of points he was accumulating. When he had earned fifty of them, he could turn in the points for a reward chosen from a menu of reinforcers. He chose to go to the zoo, but he could have chosen a later bedtime for one weekend, a model airplane, extra desserts for two nights, the chance to sit in the front of the car for two weeks, or permission to have two friends over for dinner.

Mrs. Ryan worked with Tommy's strengths instead of his weaknesses. There were times when he acted like a baby during his reading sessions, especially at the beginning, when he was afraid of his work. His mother wisely ignored these times. The babyishness subsided as he grew more confident of his own skills and realized he could get his reinforcers only by working for them.

3. *Evaluate.* The combination of individual attention, encouragement, praise, a systematic curriculum, and a point system proved successful. The records soon indicated that Tommy was reading a page from a third-grade reader in three minutes and making mistakes on fewer than one out of every ten words on the page. Mrs. Ryan kept the program going because she was confident she was on the right track. Tommy even began to read on his own.

There are several good academic (remedial) programs available commercially that a parent can use with a child. These programs have quite explicit teaching manuals, and some of them even have instructions for setting up reinforcement programs in conjunction with the academic material. We recommend those published by E & B Press, P.O. Box 10549, Eugene, Oregon 97401.

Of course it would be so much easier if the teacher could work with the child. In all fairness, though, it is hard for a teacher with thirty children to devote enough time to one child to have him or her catch up without any extra help. Many teachers do it, however, and that should be your first resource. Many schools also provide remedial programs, and you can request that your child be included in one. If the school doesn't have a program, the teacher might suggest other teachers who would be willing to work with your child.

Self-disparaging Remarks

It is a joyous feeling when a child comes home from school with a sparkle in his eyes and a growing sense of his own abilities. Unfortunately, a child sometimes comes home looking defeated and saying, "I'm stupid" or "All the others kids in the class got their third-grade books, and I have trouble with the primer." Find out what you can do specifically to help the child. It's important to talk about feelings, but it's not always best to follow self-disparaging remarks with a lengthy conversation. That can sometimes reinforce these feelings. If the child continually brings up the subject, he may be trying to provoke a reaction from you. Often it's better to ignore his self-disparaging remarks. If your words don't work the first two or three times, they probably won't work the tenth time either.

This might be a good time to show him the papers you've saved so he can see the progress he's made. He'll learn he can get more of your attention for the good things he says about himself and the good things he does than for self-deprecation. If his grades are low and you feel he could do better in school, work with him and/or his teacher to build a program in which he can be successful. Build an incentive into the program to keep him working at it. After a while you can drop the incentive program, and the feelings of success he gets from his school work will be motivation enough.

At other times you can help a child gain perspective on herself by asking her to list all her good qualities. If she can't tell you any, tell her what you like about her. Agree with all the good things she says about herself. Also praise her a lot when she shows initiative or humor or anything else positive.

Test-anxiety

Some children do very poorly on tests even though they know the work. Many, many children work themselves into a state of anxiety before a test. First find out why the child is so anxious. You can get a lot of information just by asking her what the problem is and then standing back and listening. You can also find out a lot by going over her papers with her. You can supplement this information through a teacher conference. Talking with other parents also helps in gaining perspective. The teacher might, for example, be placing too much emphasis on tests and not enough on teaching. If this is the case, let the teacher know your child's reaction. Encourage other parents to do the same; your and their children will benefit.

Letting a child know that the upcoming examination is not his one and only opportunity in this world to prove himself can also be reassuring. And of course the best way to overcome the fear of tests, or any other fear, for that matter, is to give the child the skills to master the object of the fear.

Test-taking is a skill. A number of books are available that discuss this skill, and you might want to share such a book with an older child. Another suggestion is to teach the child to read each question twice and then to answer the easy questions first, so that his anxiety has a chance to abate. Teach him to allot portions of time to each section so that he won't fear the time element in examination-taking. You can give your child some make-believe tests at home. In essay-type tests, some children find it easier to just start writing, and then organize their material later; others find it easier to first organize and then write. Discuss with your child the different ways to take an exam. Help him experiment until he finds the best way for him. And advise a child to reward himself by doing something he likes after studying hard or doing well on a test.

Misbehavior in School

If a child has had a long history of misbehavior in school, you are probably not going to change him overnight. But if you are systematic and resourceful, he can change. Let's use Kenneth as an example.

Kenneth was eleven. All his teachers said he was quite bright and was very talented in art. In social studies he was an outstanding student; he could build model villages that were the envy of much older children and even of his teachers. However, he had a history of temper outbursts. He had had a run-in with nearly every teacher in the school. There were periods when he was in trouble every day and almost every hour. Nobody quite knew why he did it, but everyone always knew what he did. Eventually Kenneth was transferred to a special-needs classroom because he swore at his teacher, and she would no longer tolerate him in class.

A behavioral program was set up for Kenneth. His special-needs teacher made up a chart with thirty boxes, each corresponding to a period of the day. It looked like this:

	M	T	W	Th	F
1st					
2nd					
3rd					
4th					
5th					
6th					

Each period in which Kenneth behaved satisfactorily was marked with a yes. Each period in which his behavior was unsatisfactory was marked with a no. For the first week the teacher kept a record for himself of Kenneth's behavior. He received ten no's.

Ken's teacher then invited the parents in for a conference. He suggested they make a deal with Kenneth, and they agreed. They told Kenneth he was starting out with a clean slate and that they expected him to do better in school. They did not expect things to change overnight, but they expected an improvement each week, if only a slight one.

Kenneth loved models and art. His parents told him he could earn one model for each week in which fewer no's appeared on the chart than in the week before. And his teacher would reward him with two extra art periods each week. Kenneth replied with abusive language. He let everyone know that he was going to do what he wanted to do, when he wanted to do it; and he didn't care what they did.

Everyone ignored the outburst, and Kenneth was assured that the deal was still on. His parents bought a model, one that he had wanted very much, and placed it on a shelf. They told him he could have it as soon as he received nine or fewer no's in a week.

The first week, Kenneth had twelve no's. When he came home on

Friday, he asked if he might have the model. His parents replied that his teacher had called, as he had said he would, and told them how many no's Kenneth had. Ken had another temper tantrum, which his parents again ignored.

The following week Kenneth had nine no's. He got the model and the extra art periods. The following week he had only eight outbursts, and the rewards followed. By this time Kenneth was becoming very conscious of his teacher's marking system. A look from the teacher was sufficient to tell Ken he was getting close to the line of misbehavior.

Within two months he was down to four no's a week. Those were the result of his behavior during lunch and recess, two of the most difficult times for children because these periods are unstructured and unsupervised. The adults began to analyze with Kenneth the problems in those situations. They found that Kenneth found it very hard to say "I'm sorry" when he accidentally bumped into someone or dropped a tray. They also found that he had great difficulty backing out of some challenges. They rehearsed with Kenneth when and how to say "I'm sorry." These two words alone got Ken out of some difficult situations.

He was also taught how to be assertive—that is, to stand up for his rights without being aggressive. If Ken was teased, for example, he was taught to tell people firmly that he didn't want to be treated that way but that he would not get himself into trouble by fighting. If he was excluded from a ball game, he was taught how to ask to be included. They also rehearsed strategies for staying away from one group of kids with whom he periodically got into trouble. By the end of the semester Ken was doing dramatically better in school.

Sometimes a child acquires a reputation that becomes self-perpetuating. "Class clown" is one of them. Some children continue to clown despite the admonitions of teachers and parents because they get so much support from their peers. Besides, it is a role they know and feel comfortable with, and sometimes they lack the ability to relate to children and teachers any other way. But they can be taught new skills through role-playing. A clever teacher (or a teacher who has received help from a clever parent) can change the system so that the class gets a vested interest in seeing the child change her behavior.

Martha Ann was eight. She was funny to everyone but her teacher. He tried hard to appreciate her, but he felt it was inappropriate for him to have to compete with her for the class's attention. He spoke to her about it, but it was hard for her to stop. The wisecracks kept pouring out, and the class kept egging her on. Sometimes she felt used by the kids.

The teacher called in Martha and her father for a three-way conference. Her father suggested that the class be given a party when Martha had cut her joking down to no more than four or five wisecracks a day. Martha agreed to quit clowning. The teacher said he would keep records: every time Martha made a wisecrack, he simply would put a check mark next to her name.

The next day the teacher told the class what had transpired at the conference. The next time Martha joked, the class gave her dirty looks, and the teacher put a check next to her name. Her remarks no longer seemed so funny. Within a short time she had stopped the wisecracking. The class had the party.

Difficulty Getting Along with Teachers

What about the child who finds it difficult to get along with the teacher? In such a case a careful investigation is always in order. There is little to be gained by belittling the teacher in front of the child. There are times, of course, when a child can't fight his or her own battles, but if he is encouraged to do so, and to suffer the consequences of his own mistakes, he will learn more and will feel more competent.

On the other hand, you can and should discuss with a child what the difficulty is and what can be done to alleviate it. Children need help in working with certain teachers. With practice and some good reinforcers, they can become skilled in using behavior modification to change other people's behavior. Plenty of reinforcers are available to them; they just need to learn how to use them. Teachers are just as receptive to positive reinforcement as anyone else.

Teach your child to make eye contact with the teacher and to nod appropriately during a lecture or discussion. Have her say openly, "I can learn so much better when you tell me some of the good things I do." Have her praise the teacher explicitly after an interesting and productive lesson. Such simple statements as "I understand that lesson perfectly now" or "Aha, now I get it!" are good for a teacher's morale, and a teacher will probably have good feelings about the person who praises her. But practice this with the child so it does not smack of artificiality. Help her do it in a convincing way.

Role-play a few of these sequences with your child to show him or her how to make positive comments. At the same time, work with your child on how to break eye contact during a scolding and how to ignore provocative remarks. Let her know that she has some power too. Teach her that she can also use these same behavioral methods with the other children in the class.

This method has been used successfully by psychologists and special-education teachers to help children get along better in school.

Special Education

Suppose a teacher tells you that your child requires a special program. Be aware that he or she is probably only making a suggestion. You can fight against arbitrary placement, as school officials well know. Don't get flustered; find out how much merit there is to the suggestion. Find out specifically why the teacher thinks so. Just as important, find out what has been done to alleviate the problem. Unless the steps that were taken were very concrete, my recommendation is to postpone any discussion of special-class placement.

There is nothing inherently either good or bad about special-class placement. Sometimes it is a wise course to follow, because the child can achieve success in relation to his or her classmates, but it can be harmful because of the stigma or because of the expectations involved.

The school will probably suggest testing. Usually the school provides the tester. If the school has not provided a systematic program to overcome the difficulties, complete with records, insist that that be done before you allow any testing. Ask that goals be set up for the child—concrete goals of reducing temper tantrums or progressing through curricular materials—and that systematic records of progress be kept. If you have any questions at all about the bias or the competence of the school psychologist, you can always get an independent evaluation.

Keep on top of the situation. Ask for a consultation with the school psychologist or learning disabilities teacher, and see if you can find out specifically what the child's difficulties are. Ask what you can do and ask to see the child's records every week. There are a lot of theories and few answers in psychology, so take things with a grain of salt. I would especially insist that people speak English instead of psychological jargon.

Be leery of any labels the professionals attach to your child. Labels are not very helpful for teaching or parenting. Don't allow a label to place a ceiling on your child's ability to learn.

Every test result and every label should be followed by two questions: "So what?" and "What do I do now?" People used to believe that retardation and emotional disturbances were permanent conditions. We know better now. Behavioral psychologists generally question the usefulness of concepts and terms like "retarded" and "disturbed." Retardation and disturbance exist in the eye of the beholder. It has been well documented that many children are retarded for only six hours a day; on the streets they are indistinguishable from their classmates. Most special-education children would be better off without the label, for the way the world reacts to a child who runs around the room and has temper tantrums is different from the way it reacts to a child who is called schizophrenic, even though the label may have been earned for running around a room and throwing a temper tantrum.

The basic question is, "What will special-class placement do for my child and at what cost?" There are no pat answers.

The U.S. Government has compiled a regional list of resources for special education which you can obtain by writing Project Closer Look, P.O. Box 1976, Washington, D.C. 20201. If you state the problem, they will tell you where help can be found. But perhaps the best advice is to talk with parents of children in the special-education program (and the children too), for they are the ones who know the pluses and minuses best.

Whether or not the child is in a special-education class, it is important that you keep abreast of developments in the classroom through the child's reports and through direct communication with the school. Be positive and encouraging in general, and when necessary use specific behavioral programs. Your working closely with your child's school needs not only helps the youngster directly, it encourages the teacher to do his or her best too.

CHAPTER X

Socialization

People are social beings. They need one another and they need to get along with one another. They first learn how to do this during childhood. The initial lessons come in infancy, but every year is important. The family is the place were socialization begins.

This chapter will discuss the family and ways to increase positive behavior between brothers and sisters. It will also take up ways of helping a child who is very shy or very active.

Interaction within the Family

Families have many functions. Ideally, the family provides a warm, nurturing atmosphere in which dreams and hopes are shared, where each member can grow, where all feel accepted and respected. Few families ever achieve that ideal completely, but you can make a lot of it happen by working at it. Clear, direct and open communication, the sharing of one's dreams and disappointments, can be fostered by the practices a family adopts. In an open household, inner feelings are encouraged and dealt with rather than inhibited. If Susan is having trouble with a friend or not getting along with her mother, she should feel free to bring these topics up rather than have to keep them to herself. If a child's feelings are accepted, he or she will share the problems as well as the good things. Everyone needs to do both. In addition, when a child's feelings are accepted, he or she will try to please you, just as you try to please people you love.

A key ingredient in helping children (or anyone else) grow is respect. Each person needs to be first respected for himself, then encouraged to bring out the best in himself. If each person is treated with dignity, he can accept his own mistakes and the criticism of others. He won't be overly critical of himself or of other people.

Children who feel that their dignity has been offended will try hard to get back at adults. They are too young to realize that they're getting back at themselves as well. It might be a cliché, but the best way to maintain a child's dignity is to treat him or her as you would want to be treated. If you have to be reprimanded, wouldn't you prefer that the reprimand be given privately and without rancor? Wouldn't you rather discuss the problem and ways to make it better than hear character judgments about yourself? If you treat a child as you want to be treated and show him or her that the future is still open, no matter what the present circumstances, you'll be able to teach appropriate social behavior much faster and easier.

Along with respect comes honesty. It has to be taught by example. There is a place for privacy in our lives and thoughts, and for things that we don't have to share with anyone if we don't feel like it. But deceiving a child—or other members of your family—creates an atmosphere of guardedness and self-censorship than can work against everyone. Honesty has to start with you. Work on making your house a place where no one is afraid to tell the truth—even when it's something you as the parent won't like. If problems are out in the open, they can always be dealt with; the ones that go underground cause the most difficulty. Make it possible for children to own up to mistakes or to disagree. If a child loses something or gets into trouble with a teacher, it's best to have the kind of atmosphere where he or she can tell you what happened. If a teenager is going to start smoking, it's important that he or she discuss it with you. You might not end up approving of your child's behavior, but at least you will know about it. Try to remain open to other points of view, be willing to compromise at times, and above all don't be punitive. A child has to learn that honesty pays.

The more you model the behavior you want from a child, the more readily you will see that behavior. If a child shouts at you, don't shout back. You'll get your point across more effectively by backing off and informing the child that you're not shouting at him or her and that you won't allow yourself to be shouted at either. Break off the discussion if necessary and come back to it later. Teenagers sometimes call their parents names. Let them know that you are aware that they disagree with you, but that it's more fruitful to discuss the issue at hand than to engage in name calling. Tell them that you won't call them names and in turn you don't want to be called names. Teach them a better way to say that they disagree with you or don't approve of your decision, which is really what name calling amounts to for many children.

Let your child see you as a strong, positive person who cares about her and her place in the family. Help her to identify with your family and your standards. One way to develop family identification is by doing things together, especially having fun. Play games with one another, go on trips and hikes, or visit together.

Parents should share their interests and their avocations with children so that children can learn about and do interesting things with them. It doesn't matter whether it is watching football, planting a garden, playing badminton or doing needlepoint.

Holidays and family get-togethers are important in helping children build a sense of identity with the family. Participating in preparing special family meals or planning parties can go a long way toward building a sense of family.

Children also need to be encouraged to do things. Watch a child perform in her Little League game or at a dance recital. Bring the other members of the family along so that the children learn to root for and encourage one another. Instill in everyone the idea that the obligation of a family is to encourage and help, not to berate or downgrade each other.

Cooperation is an important element in building family identity. First, though, you have to define what cooperation means in your terms. Think of what the child does or doesn't do that is cooperative as you define it. Then apply the three-step method to build cooperative behaviors and discourage their opposite.

Set your objectives at the child's level. Every time you see a child do something you consider cooperative, reinforce it. If you don't see much to reinforce, initiate something—that is, get the child to help you carry in the packages from the car and then reinforce her action. Let her know how much you appreciated her help; then make some popcorn together. Let a child know you appreciate his cooperation in playing quietly when you're working, then follow it up with something special. You can even let an infant know you appreciate her holding still while you change her diapers. She won't understand the words, but she'll understand the pat and the smile.

Given encouragement, little children often love to help; it makes them feel important and grown up. At the beginning, of course, it will be easier for you to do the vacuuming alone than with Colin's help, but if you are encouraging, the help will soon be real.

Chores can be set up to promote cooperation too. For example, suggest that you all clean the yard together, then go out for ice cream. Or when the cellar has been cleaned, all of you work on making it into a playroom.

Fighting among Brothers and Sisters

When brothers and sisters fight, you should try to find out why. When they are young, the reward they receive for fighting is often attention. They also resort to fighting because they lack experience in working things out any other way.

Mary, age four, had two favorite games: knocking over her older brother's block buildings and switching the TV channel during the exciting part of a program. She usually got smacked hard by her brother for her antics, but that didn't stop her. Many times her mother saved her from a merciless beating. Punishing Mary's brother didn't prevent him from hitting his sister. His mother realized he was provoked, but she didn't want him hitting Mary.

Her mother learned what Mary was getting out of her behavior when she overheard Mary saying, "I can get Mommy to punish you any time I want to." Her brother's reply was, "Her spankings don't hurt, and they're worth it, because I hate you so much."

Mother decided it was time to step out of the way. She told the children she would not interfere in their arguments anymore. The next time Mary got whacked, her mother checked her impulse to "rescue" her daughter. There were two major battles that day, but Mary began to realize there was no sense in provoking her brother, because it didn't bring about the effects she wanted.

When one child complains to you about the other one, ask the complainer what he or she intends to do about the problem. This strategy encourages children to resolve conflicts on their own, a necessary prerequisite for cooperation.

Peter came down one night complaining that his brother was scaring him. His mother asked him what he was going to do about it. After a few more futile attempts to enlist his mother's aid, he went back upstairs. His mother overheard him say to his brother, "If you won't make faces to scare me, I won't knock over your block towers anymore." His brother replied that it was a deal, and they shook on it.

If you feel you must actively intervene, set up an incentive program for the children. Teach them they can change each other's behavior by selectively ignoring and reinforcing. If Johnny provokes Mary, Mary can get the reward by ignoring Johnny. Johnny will stop provoking, because Mary will not respond and because he will lose out on the reward if she does respond. Let the children themselves work out how to get the reward.

Keep a record of the children's fights. You may discover that they don't fight nearly as much as you thought they did. In any case, you will be able to monitor any progress.

Needless to say, you should strongly reinforce cooperative behavior. Don't take it for granted. When John helps David clean his room, praise him for helping his brother and then take them both out for a treat. You can also encourage children in more explicit ways. Set up some tasks that require more than one person, such as cleaning a room or the yard.

Another suggestion is to have children give a joint party. Let them make up the guest list together, prepare the food and decorations, and clean up. The party will be a reinforcer. So will your telling them how proud you are of the job they did. When you can do so naturally, point out the benefits of sharing. A child can have the use of more books or toys if he or she is willing to share with a brother or sister.

Don't overlook the importance of games in building up brother-and-sister relationships. At the very least, games require taking turns and following rules. You can participate too by taking time to teach them some new games and by demonstrating how to give and take and to negotiate differences. Games also occupy a child's time. The more children are occupied, the less opportunity there is for fighting. Boredom brings out the worst in all of us. Invite their friends over if you think the children are fighting because of boredom, and see that their activities are varied.

You might also be able to cut down on children's fighting by making sure each child has his or her own private space, even if that space has to be marked off by a bookcase. Make it a place where no one can enter without permission. Each child should also have a place for his or her private possessions. The more one feels like an individual, the easier it is to be part of a family.

If fighting occurs in the car, it is necessary to be firm. When possible, stop driving. Let the children know that they are endangering everyone's life and that you refuse to drive under those conditions. One family that took a cross-country car trip solved the problem of fighting by keeping a minimum of food and water in the car and spacing out their rests. The children soon learned that if they wanted to eat and take a stretch they would have to cooperate.

You can also set up explicit programs like point systems, or you can tell the children that after they travel for two hours without fighting you will stop for hamburgers. Being able to ride in the front seat with the driver (taking turns here is essential) is a marvelous enticement for children to behave appropriately—and getting a favored seat also relieves their boredom.

Competition and Jealousy among Siblings

Competition is a fact of life for children. They will first compete for your attention, which is why it's always important to reserve some time for each child individually. Except for rewarding cooperation, there's little that can be done to avoid at least some competition. You can try to discourage competition indirectly, however. In our family we helped foster one girl's interest in dance and the other's in art. When our older son fell in love with skiing and announced his desire to race and jump, we encouraged the other son's interest in ice skating and hockey.

A child might claim that her brother or sister is favored over her. Discuss this topic with the child during one of the special moments before bed or while walking together. Let her express her feelings on the matter. Listen carefully. You may learn that you are doing something you were not conscious of. One child, age eight, complained that when his mother woke him and his brother, she always sat on the younger child's bed and talked only to him. When the mother realized what she was doing, she quickly corrected it.

Explain to your children your policy on buying presents or taking individual children out for special treats. It's easier to be consistent if you rotate gifts and treats. If you have been inconsistent, admit it and take steps to change. If you are satisfied that remarks about favoritism have no basis in fact, ignore them. Actions speak louder than words, so if you are fair your child will come to recognize it.

Many families have the most difficulty with jealousy when a new baby arrives on the scene. One way you can cut down on this jealousy is by showing the older child that he or she is valued. When it's time for a feeding or you're otherwise busy with the baby, ask the older child to help you. Be very reinforcing when he does. If you're feeding the baby, you can read the older child a story at the same time or talk to him. Then your spending time with the baby will become more acceptable because there will be something in it for the older child too.

If jealousy of a newborn seems to be getting out of hand, ask the older child if he wants to be like the baby. Tell him you accept his desire to be pampered and allow him to satisfy it. Let him take milk from the bottle and even climb into the crib and wear diapers if he wants. But carry it through when it comes time for feeding and sleeping. Give the child baby food. Explain matter-of-factly that babies get lots of attention and care but that there are a lot of things they can't do, one of which is eat grown-up food. The older child will soon see it's more fun to be grown up.

If an older child feels jealous of a younger one, point out the privileges and responsibilities that age and competence bring. Ask him if he would like to switch roles. If he agrees, exempt him from the snow shoveling but have him go to bed at the younger child's bedtime. Serve him small portions and insist that he play in the yard instead of going out in the street. He will soon discover that there is a real payoff for being competent, and that extra responsibilities also bring extra privileges. If the younger child is the one complaining, you might point out the extra responsibilities the older one has to shoulder. Tell the younger one you'll always be happy to discuss his earning a later bedtime or permission to play in the street when he demonstrates that he can do his present jobs well (which might include getting along better with his brothers and sisters).

Rotating jobs and privileges is one way to ensure that children are treated fairly. If they take turns using the bathroom first or choosing the Sunday night TV programs, they will have far less to fight about.

Getting Along with Others

The best way to help children learn to get along with others is to encourage them to work out their own solutions to their problems. Even little children can learn this. If a child comes crying to you that Sarah threw sand at him, ask him what he is going to do about it. One suggestion might be to stay far away from her. Another might be for your child to say, "I won't play with you if you do that." Discuss alternatives with the youngster, then let the child exercise his own judgment and find out what he can do to control or change the situation. You will have to impose limitations sometimes as well as give suggestions, but by and large children have to fight their own battles.

Children will sometimes try to play one parent against the other by reporting how badly they were mistreated by the other. This happens most often in the teens, and it can be devastating to a family if the child is successful. Sometimes a son will go to a mother, for example, and explain how unreasonable his father is. The mother will listen sympathetically and agree, or she will tell the child that she will try to get her husband to change his mind or behave differently about a particular situation. In the long run that only exacerbates the problem, as the son gets support for his hostility toward his father, and the father, feeling isolated and jealous, then tries to get back at his son and his wife. A preferable alternative is for the mother to listen and then, without taking sides, ask the son what he intends to do about his problem.

This is not to say that children don't need help and instruction in dealing with other people. Children may have to be taught how to be assertive or when to ignore a situation. They may have to learn skills like how to fight or how to write an acceptable paper for an English teacher. Above all they need to know that you're on their side and that you think they're capable of handling problems themselves. If you really believe it, eventually they will be.

The Shy Child

All young children find it difficult to get along with strangers, but some children have more difficulty than others. There are several ways of helping a shy child make friends and get along with people.

If your child reacts strongly to strangers, advise strangers to hold back and let the child approach them instead of the other way around. Let them know that the child might let them hold her later on, but first she has to get used to them. If the child is older, suggest to a visitor that the child would be more apt to approach him and sit on his lap if he would hold a book open so she could see the pictures.

Shy children need some extra help in making friends, adapting to change, and speaking up in front of strangers. One way to start is to provide the child with someone to play with, even if the child does not react positively at first. Invite other parents and their children over for coffee and play. A shy child has to slowly acclimate himself to other children. Even if your child is reluctant to play, at least he can get used to being with other children.

Your child might cling to you or retire to a corner. Accept that at first. After a while, perhaps several visits, try to draw him out. Use your attention selectively—that is, pay the most attention to your child when he is playing with or near the other child. Set up the games and toys near both children. Play with both, one at a time if necessary. Roll a ball first to one child, then to the other. Eventually make it a three-sided game (four-sided if the other parent wants to play too). If your child walks away, ignore him. If he comes back, lavish a lot of attention on him. After you have all played together for even a few minutes you can serve the children ice cream. Besides reinforcing the children's playing together, it will surely get them to sit together while eating.

If your child has a problem speaking up, you can enlist the aid of a friendly candystore man. When you go shopping, give the child a few pennies and let her buy some treats with them. If she just points at the candy, have the candystore man ask her in a nice way to speak up. Have him pretend he can't hear her if she just whispers.

You can also play school with her. It would be best to have a few children involved, but if you can't find any, make believe there are a few other kids in the class. Pretend you're the teacher and ask some questions. Ask the other players, real or imaginary, their names. Praise them for answering. Ask one of them to speak up, and praise the increase in volume. Then ask your child some questions you know she can answer. Be lavish in your reinforcement when she answers. Use nuts and raisins as well as words of praise to reinforce a forceful or loud voice.

If the child is a preschooler, you might consider sending her to nursery school. Nursery school provides children with an opportunity to relate to other children and to adults. They learn to play with other children, to share and take turns, and to follow some rules. Most nursery schools also provide facilities and activities that the average home cannot provide. A good nursery-school teacher can give you information as to how your son or daughter is doing and how problems can be corrected. Besides, nursery school can provide a much needed rest for parents. And it can make a child's adjustment to elementary school that much easier.

Another way you can help a shy child is through hiring new babysitters once in a while so that the child gets used to new faces and new activities. If you have a teenager who is shy, encourage him or her to babysit. Shy adolescents often feel more comfortable with younger children.

There are other ways you can help a shy child gain friends and/or learn to interact with others. Day camps are sometimes very good in this respect. They are often low-pressure and let a child go at his or her own pace. At the same time they bring the youngster into contact with other children of the same age. Some communities have family picnics where there are, of course, lots of children around; these too can get a child playing with other children.

Public places, in fact, provide excellent opportunities to meet other children. Thus, a public beach is preferable to a swimming hole or a private beach. Ice skating at the lake and joining the local pool are other possibilities. Spend a fair amount of time with your child, but don't end up feeling you have to spend all your time with him. You are entitled to your own friends too, and the child's boredom might just provide him or her with the motivation to go off with another child to play or talk.

If the child is in school, encourage him or her to join clubs or Cub Scouts or Brownies. In some cases it might be advisable not to put joining up for discussion. Often shy children need that extra gentle push. Let the child know that he will have to stay with the group for a given period of time. You should be willing to discuss continued participation, of course, after that time.

It can also help to develop a child's special skill, whether it is in art, sports or any other area. The child will then be more likely to join in sports or creative activities.

The Overactive Child

By and large it is best to accept a child's temperament, but it is important to train a very active child to slow down a little and pay more attention to tasks. There are many ways to reinforce behaviors that are incompatible with restlessness and physical motion.

Barbara, age four, was diagnosed as hyperactive. Her parents asked the pediatrician for a specific program. The pediatrician suggested treasure hunts as a means of getting Barbara to listen. They were to start off with simple directions: "Take the kitchen chair over to the cabinet. Climb on the chair and open the door. Look behind the soup cans and you will find a surprise." As Barbara began to listen better, the directions became more complicated.

The parents were also advised to read to Barbara. Whenever they pronounced the name of the main character, if Barbara raised her hand she was to get some nuts. Another suggestion was to watch TV with Barbara.

You can play active games with an overactive child, but make them games that inhibit movement. Barbara's parents played "statues" with her. In this game the players run and jump and are as active as they can be—until "It" cries out, "Freeze!" Then all players have to freeze, no matter what position they are in, and stay that way for ten seconds. This can be gradually increased to one minute.

Another game is Red Light–Green Light. In this game "It" turns his back to the players. When he says, "Green light," the players advance toward the base as quickly as they can. On the command "Red light," "It" turns around and everyone has to stop where he is no matter what position he is in. If a person is caught moving on a red light, he or she has to go back to the starting line. The game continues until someone tags "It"; then the game can be started again.

When you play a game with your child, be sure to keep it a game. If the child walks away, it's because he or she is not having any fun. Don't holler at the child or get angry. Just change your style or simplify the rules so the child will want to play.

Barbara's parents used mealtimes as an occasion for training her to sit still. At first, Barbara would take one bite and then leave the table. This she did repeatedly until the meal was over. Her parents told her she had to take two bites before she could get up. Barbara could easily comply with that. Then they required her to eat a little more at a time until she could eat half the main course at one sitting. Finally they required her to eat at least half the meal before leaving the table. If she failed to sit still for a specific length of time, they cleared her plate. At the next meal, her hunger motivated her to sit through a good part of the meal. Within two months she was able to sit through the entire meal.

They then prolonged the meal by asking her questions and riddles between the main course and the dessert. The questions were easy and fun and she liked to play. Some typical questions were "Who is taller, Mommy or Daddy?" "Who is older, you or your brother?" "What color is your shirt?"

Before bedtime they played games together, making them into a ritual. One game they played was Concentration. Her father laid out five items on a blanket and asked Barbara to look closely at the items, then close her eyes while he took one away. She then had to tell which item was missing. Every time she gave the right answer, he gave her some popcorn. As she got better at it, her father increased the number of items on the blanket. He began giving her four pieces of popcorn for getting it right the first time and only two pieces for getting it the second time.

By the time Barbara entered school she was capable of sitting for relatively long periods of time, concentrating on tasks, and asking and answering questions as well as following directions. As far as everyone was concerned, she had outgrown her period of hyperactivity. It took time and a lot of effort, and it wasn't always fun, but it paid off in school.

Be sure to accentuate what the child does right instead of dwelling on his mistakes. Set up your program so that it is possible for the child to succeed, and then reinforce even the minutest progress. Help build the child's self-image as well.

Marvin, age eight, was one of those children who seldom completed a task. His teacher gave him a nearly completed puzzle, one that required only a few pieces to complete. She worked with Marvin, and then let him put in the final piece by himself. Then she complimented him on his puzzle-solving ability. The next day the teacher left out a few more pieces, and while Marvin was working on the puzzle the teacher praised him for his persistence. Marvin liked that word when he found out what it meant. The teacher called Marvin persistent whenever she legitimately could. Marvin kept on working hard to earn the compliment and eventually was able to complete the puzzle on his own.

It is important not to expect instantaneous results with this approach. Progress can be slow and problems of this kind can try your patience. But if you keep rewarding improvement, you yourself will eventually be rewarded—with success.

Finally, it may give you perspective to realize that every child has some kind of social difficulty at one time or another. Think back to your own childhood. The likelihood is that, barring serious social maladjustment, the child will eventually grow out of it. It takes time as well as effort to learn how to get along with others.

CHAPTER XI

Social Problems

Some children need to be helped to give up behaviors that will interfere with their social development. This chapter will examine how parents can help children in this regard. Specifically, it discusses methods of decreasing tantrums, lying, stealing, inappropriate sex play, rudeness, whining, excessive crying, argumentativeness and rebelliousness. Thumb-sucking, nail-biting, tics, excessive scratching, carrying around blankets, and rocking are also discussed, though the point is made that at least some of these behaviors will not be a problem to the child if they are not a problem to you.

Tantrums

The surest way to eliminate tantrums is to ignore them. Admittedly, this is not as simple as it sounds. It's one thing to ignore a tantrum in the privacy of your own home, but it's a lot more difficult—and embarrassing—to do it in a crowded department store. You don't have to walk out of the store, but you can gather Johnny or Mary Jane under one arm and take the child to a semi-private place. The message always has to be the following: you can *never* get your way by behaving like that; I will always be willing to talk with you, but I will *not* give in to that kind of behavior.

Tantrums often come about when children balk at parental "commands," such as "Take a bath" or "You cannot take Mommy's tennis racket outside." Motivating the child beforehand can avert the necessity for commands.

A little bubble bath sometimes lures a child into the bathtub (though it should be a small amount—too much soap can be painful to the urethra, particularly for girls); a tubful of plastic toys and boats almost always does. Humor often works: after filling the tub with lukewarm water, toys and bubble bath, tell the child kiddingly, "You can't take a bath. Absolutely not." Joke around as you help the child undress and get into the bath. Sometimes you have to physically guide a young child along. The moment the youngster moves in the desired direction, ease your pressure.

If the child still throws tantrums, give him or her the bath anyway. That way the child learns that baths are to be taken every evening, even if he cries. But during the struggles be as tender and reassuring as possible. Try to distract the child from his crying. Sometimes a well-placed question and reinforcer—"Do you want to make chocolate pudding with me after the bath?"—or an announcement about who is coming to visit tomorrow will dry tears almost immediately. When the tears have stopped, compliment the youngster on how big he is for being able to stop crying so fast. Then try to get the child to have fun and show you he can swim in the tub.

When a child discovers that she has to listen to you and that she cannot control you through tantrums, those tantrums will diminish. They require a lot of energy; why expend it if you can't get your own way? And of course the more you build the bath into a routine, the more readily the child will accept it as a part of life.

You could also tie explicit rewards to finishing the bath in an appropriate manner. "When you have finished the bath, then we can make fudge or read a story." The child can also accumulate points for taking baths in a more mature manner. So many points might mean a later bedtime or sitting in the front seat of the car or satisfying some other desire. You can also tie rewards to a reduction of tantrums. Just keep a count of how many occur each day. Reward the child when there are fewer tantrums over a given time period. When baths become routine, you will be able to discontinue the rewards.

What about the tantrum that follows the refusal of a request? Again, ignoring is the best solution. At the same time it's important to teach children alternative ways of behaving. Let's suppose your child wants to take your tennis racket outside to use as a baseball bat, and you tell her she can't do that. Then she has a tantrum.

If she's little enough, pick her up and put her in her room. Let her know you're available to talk when she settles down. Set a timer and tell her she can come out in fifteen minutes. If she's too old to pick up, just walk away from the tantrum. Be sure, though, that the child doesn't take the racket outside; put it away before you exit. As you leave, announce that you'll be available to talk after you've finished your bath or chore.

When the child has calmed down, discuss the incident. Tell her she could have saved herself a lot of effort by asking you what could take the place of the racket. Children should be encouraged to explore alternative ideas when one doesn't work out. Reinforce her ideas about how to get around obstacles in a constructive way. At the same time emphasize that "no" means no.

Almost every child goes through a stage of throwing tantrums. The lucky ones find there's no reward for having a tantrum. The unlucky ones find it rewarding enough to continue. Then they meet people—teachers, for example—who are not so indulgent, and have to learn the hard way to behave in an age-appropriate manner.

Unfortunately, older children have temper tantrums too (not to mention some adults). These are a lot harder to ignore. An incentive system, based on a reduction of tantrums, can help.

Dora, a twelve-year-old, had a long history of tantrums that were causing enormous problems in the family. Dora even admitted she didn't like what she did, but sometimes she lost control of herself. Her parents discussed the problem with a psychologist. At his suggestion they asked Dora what it would take to help her stop her tantrums. Dora said she wanted a puppy, something they had always refused her.

All three sat down with the psychologist and worked out an agreement. Dora could have the dog under two conditions: one, she had to earn it; two, she had to take care of it.

Dora could get the dog in thirteen weeks—i.e., by Christmas. In order to earn the dog, she had to have fewer than sixty-five points. Points—demerits, actually—were accumulated through temper tantrums. The number sixty-five was based on the number of tantrums she had had in previous weeks. (The parents knew the number because, on the psychologist's advice, they had kept records.)

A distinction was made between arguing and temper tantrums. Tantrums were defined as speaking in a voice so loud it could be heard two rooms away, saying the same things over and over, and insulting the parents. Arguing was actually encouraged as part of the family therapy, since it was felt that Dora did not know how to stand up for her rights in an appropriate way and was not skilled at expressing her reasons for wanting or not wanting something.

Each tantrum cost Dora three points, but if she stopped herself within two minutes, it cost her only one point. If a tantrum started, Dora's parents had to tell her to stop, and then they had to walk away for two minutes. If Dora had stopped when they came back, it was only a one-point tantrum.

They all figured out ways for Dora to avert her anger. Arguing and making her views known was one way. Dora herself suggested (and came to use this technique a great deal) that when she felt a tantrum coming on, she would hold her breath, turn around, and tell everyone she wanted some time to calm down. She learned to stay STOP to herself and pinch herself when she felt she was losing control. Dora also said she would try to think of the puppy whenever she was starting to get angry.

The system was successful—after thirteen weeks Dora had decreased her tantrums, and she had learned that she could control herself.

Lying

Little children don't lie; they just don't know what is meant by the truth. If a youngster says she caught 4,000 fish, she's not lying. She is simply confusing fantasy and reality. It is only later, as words come to mean the same to a child as they do to an adult, that a child actually lies.

Many preschool children invent imaginary companions. They outgrow this phase, so don't make a big deal out of it. You can play along with your child's fantasy if you wish, or you can ignore the whole thing. Sometimes you might not even know about it until the nursery-school teacher asks you how your son is, and you find out that your daughter has invented a brother named Harry. Children who get into trouble often invent imaginary friends who "make" them get into difficulty. Sometimes they treat the imaginary friend in a manner similar to the way you treat them, so watch and listen—you might learn a lot about yourself.

What if the child is older and doesn't tell the truth? First, it's important to recognize that most of us at one time or another have lied either to get ourselves out of a tight spot or because tact called for a stretching of the truth. Don't be too hard on a child—don't demand that he meet standards that we sometimes cannot meet ourselves.

Ask yourself why a child lies. Does she do it with full knowledge beforehand that she will be caught in the lie? If so, the child is asking for attention, and it's important that you give it to her. But be sure to hinge it on a child's honest behavior, rather than her dishonest troublesome actions. Ask yourself also if the punishment for transgressions is so harsh that the youngster has learned it's better to lie than to be punished. Many children lie because they are afraid to tell the truth. The best and probably the only way to give a child respect for truth is to teach him that honesty pays.

Punishment for lying should not be harsh. Try to tie the punishment naturally to what the child lied about. If he broke a window, for example, and denied it or blamed someone else, have him pay for the window. Let him know, too, that you have no respect for lying. Even if you can understand it, you cannot condone it. At the same time, try to convey to the child that you and he can work anything out, even though you can't promise it will always go his way or be pleasant.

Try to determine whether there's too much pressure on a child. If he lies about his school work, it might mean he is unable to do it and can't face admitting it to anyone. It is important for the child to understand that it is not necessary to lie if one is having difficulties, and that lying usually brings on more difficulties. Urging a child to tell you what the problem is and offering suggestions on what can be done to correct it is a hundred times more effective than harping on honesty. The child may also be subject to the pressure of other children to engage in behavior that does not meet your standards or the school's—or you may be expecting too much from him.

Stealing

A child under the age of three has a great deal of difficulty distinguishing between his or her property and someone else's. "Mine" is usually thought of as what I have plus what you have but I want to own. It's best to handle the taking of another child's toys or other possessions with a gentle reminder that Mary needs her toy back; it's hers and she wants to play with it. Remind her that she has her own toys to play with. After a while a child will learn to differentiate between what actually belongs to her and what she wants.

Most children at one time or another will take something that doesn't belong to them. Often it's money from your purse or change left on the dresser. Deal with this firmly. Let the child know unceremoniously that there are such things as private property and private places. (Of course, for this to have meaning to a child, it is necesary that the child have his or her own private space and possessions.) Let the youngster know that taking away others' possessions is entirely unacceptable. Insist on immediate restitution. If something was taken from a store, let the child hand it back to the owner. The child will feel a certain amount of humiliation, and that is to the good. But don't leave the child with the feeling he or she will never be loved again. Reassure him that although you strongly disapprove of his action, you have not stopped loving him.

When a school-age child steals, it's a more serious matter. Ask yourself why the child is stealing. Very often a child will steal for thrills. It is important to let her know very bluntly what you think of that. Try to channel these energies into sports or some other activity. Sometimes a child will take money to buy treats for friends. Again, the child must be treated firmly and forced to make restitution. Let her earn money doing jobs around the house or for someone else.

Sex Play

Children learn very early in life that sex is powerful. They learn that their sexuality affords them great pleasure, and that it can provoke a rise from other people. Guiding a child into a healthy and satisfying course with sex is a difficult task, one that sets off conflicting feelings in parents. Most adults would like children to learn that sex is pleasurable and good. On the other hand, they want children to learn to control their impulses and practice sex the "right" way. Eventually everyone has to find his or her own "right" way, but children need guidance in this area. They need to avoid social penalties and their own bad feelings about what they do with sex.

All children stimulate their genitals. At an early age they discover that this brings them pleasure, and initially they are not aware of societal sanctions. Making a big to-do over masturbation is not going to stop it. The child needs to be taught that there are times and places for genital stimulation and that the living room and the park are not those places. You can get this across though discussion, diversion, and reinforcement of activities incompatible with masturbation.

Later, as children begin to socialize with other children, another kind of problem arises. How do you handle children who play doctor or are continually trying to see their friends' genitals?

There are no pat answers. In the long run I believe it is healthiest if a parent firmly, but not punitively, informs the child that she doesn't approve of that type of play (if you don't), and that sex is a private matter. The sex play might still go on (in fact it undoubtedly will), but at least the child will become more aware of the need for discretion.

Out of a sense of daring more than anything else, some children will urinate in the most outlandish places. They will pull down their pants in school or in some other inappropriate place, or even stand by the side of the road and expose themselves when a car passes by. This is not a perversion or a sign of deep-seated maladjustment in a young child. It has to be handled, of course, but you don't want to leave the youngster with the feeling that he or she is "bad." Rather, you want the child to learn that there are appropriate and inappropriate ways to behave in this world, and that there are a lot of rules governing sexual conduct.

Treat those behaviors firmly, but not any differently than you would treat excessive rudeness or other behaviors you want to see brought under control. Let the child know in no uncertain terms that you disapprove of a particular behavior and why. Explain that in the long run such behavior is self-defeating, because it will prevent the child from making good friends and because other people will find it offensive. Send a child to his or her room to emphasize your disapproval. Put it in terms of "when children behave immaturely they have to be treated like much younger children."

At the same time, ask yourself why the child is doing this. Is it the desire to be noticed or to have limits placed on him? Devote most of your attention to the things a child does right, and don't become overly concerned with the misbehavior. Gradually the child will learn to accept your standards, at least until he can set his own.

It is also important that children have basic information about sex. Encourage children to take part in sex discussions sponsored by the school, community organizations, and your church.

Rudeness

The best way to prevent a child from being rude is to teach him or her good manners. The purpose behind manners (social customs) is to make people feel good, or at least at ease. When you say "thank you" to a person, you let him know you appreciate his efforts. When you say "hi" to a person, you let her know you're friendly. That sense of communication needs to be conveyed to a child as well as the particulars of what to do and say in specific situations.

Manners are often first taught around the dinner table. It's a perfect place to learn how and when to say "thank you," "please" and "you're welcome," as well as whether to use a fork or fingers.

The Smiths were embarrassed to have their friends over for dinner. The probem was the children's table manners. The parents decided to concentrate on three behaviors: cleaning up before dinner without having to be reminded, using utensils properly, and getting along at the dinner table. The parents set up a when-then program with the children. As soon as the children accomplished what was expected, each child would be able to invite one friend over for dinner. The plan worked perfectly.

Other areas that can be worked on in a similar fashion are passing things properly, chewing with mouths closed (if that is valued), and placing utensils and elbows in the proper places. There are also skills involved in pouring, cutting food "properly," etc., and these need to be learned. So do routines—getting to meals on time, leaving meals at the right time, and so forth. All of these can be taught through the three-step method.

A few other points: keep portions small and keep conversation flowing around the dinner table. The more a youngster is engaging in conversation and enjoying a meal, the less time there is for horseplay and fooling with food. Children are quite observant—you will find your boy or girl eventually picking up your manner of eating and speaking. They will learn more from your example than from your verbal instructions. And of course the more careful you are to note and reinforce good manners, the more frequently your child will practice them.

You can also have fun with manners. Teach a child to say "thank you" in ten different languages. Make it into a family project to find out how different people say "thank you" (*gracias, merci,* etc.) and whatever else you can think of. Do the same with "you're welcome" and with greetings. Even teenagers like this activity.

When teaching manners, it is important to work on one behavior at a time. Keep after that behavior until it becomes automatic, and then start on another. Let's specifically discuss teaching a child how to say "thank you" after receiving a gift.

Be explicit with the youngster: "When somebody gives you something, you should say, 'thank you.' That makes the person feel good about helping you, because it shows him you appreciate what he did. Everybody likes to be appreciated when he does something for someone." Model what to say—and how to say it—for the child. When the child repeats the phrases she's learned from you, thank her. Tell the youngster how proud you are of her. You might have to add extra instructions, such as "Look the person in the eye when you thank him," or "Say it loud enough so he can hear you." Give the children feedback as to what they do right as well as what needs to be improved on.

Give reminders beforehand if necessary. Usually your modeling and the child's desire to please you will be sufficient to motivate the child. It not, tie another reinforcer to those phrases.

Company manners can also be taught through direct instruction. Role-playing can show the child what to do. For example, Jane's parents had guests who dropped by for a drink. When they left they said goodbye to Jane, but she was so engrossed in a TV program that she merely nodded to them as they were leaving. The company didn't even see her nod.

Jane's father told her that he appreciated how polite she had been to the company, but that he wished she had stood up, looked their neighbors in the eye and said, "Goodbye. Thanks for coming. Please come again." Jane's father explained to her why he thought that was important. He had her play the part of the guest who said goodbye, and he played her part. He stood, looked her in the eye and spoke directly to her, inviting her back again. The father then asked Jane to do it. He praised what she did right but suggested that she speak up more. They repeated the interchange. Then he thanked her for learning so fast, and let it go at that.

The next time the company came, he built on what she could already do. Slowly, she became aware of cultural demands. He could have put the behaviors that made up politeness on a point system, but he felt it wasn't necessary. With young children it seldom is. It's often a question of their knowing what to do.

Children often misbehave in front of visitors because they feel excluded, so it's usually helpful to include the child in some of the interactions with company. Be straightforward about when their presence is welcome and when it is not. You might mention to the children that when they have friends over and are in the middle of a game, you don't interrupt them, and that you expect the same courtesy to be extended to you. On the other hand, they are welcome to come down for dessert, or they can help serve the hors d'oeuvres and then eat some of the potato chips. The chips, the desire to help, plus the chance to satisfy their own curiosity as to what grownups talk about, can be quite reinforcing.

Growth in this area can be evaluated through a chart that lists appropriate and inappropriate behavior. For example, a chart might look like this:

Company Manners: One-Month Chart

Saying thanks					
Greetings					
Table manners					
Quiet play					

Simply put a "yes" in a box for good manners and a "no" for inappropriate manners. If you decide to attach a reward to appropriate manners, the record will clearly show whether or not the reward was earned.

There will be times when a child doesn't say "thank you," either because he forgets or because he doesn't feel like it. A child might be disappointed, for example, that Johnny brought him a coloring book instead of a ball for his birthday. Helping a child to say "thank you" on such an occasion might be considered surface manners, but it's the stuff of which consideration and sensitivity are built. Let the child know matter-of-factly that it is too bad he is disappointed, but it doesn't change things, and there's no point in hurting Johnny's feelings in the bargain. Johnny tried to please, and that's what matters. Teaching your child to appreciate the thought as well as the gift may take a long time, but eventually he will learn to do it.

If your child is slow in learning these skills, you can set up an explicit system. First, be specific about what you want to teach, and let the child know why you think it is important. The manners you might want to teach might include the following: saying "thank you," "you're welcome," "excuse me," and "I'm sorry"; taking off your hat inside a building; greeting a person appropriately.

Tell children how and when to use these behaviors. Role-play if necessary. Every time a child uses one of those phrases appropriately, give her a gold star or place an X in the desired-behavior column. Tie a reward to an increase in polite manners, or take the child with you to a special place. Let her know you are going there because she earned it, and that now that she is so polite, it is a real pleasure to take her with you.

Whining

Children learn to whine because they get their own way, at least part of the time, by annoying you. If you gave in all the time, the child would have no need to whine; if you seldom changed your mind, whining would not develop. If a child has been whining for years, you can rest assured it won't stop easily, but eventually it should abate.

To help a child overcome this habit, try one or more of the following techniques.

1. Completely and consistently ignore the whining. Tell the child you intend to ignore his whining, and then keep your word. He will get the message sooner that way.

2. Set up a program to reinforce your consistency in ignoring. Give yourself a lot of little rewards—taking a bubble bath, finishing or starting a novel, running an errand (if you consider that a reward), or anything else that requires you to walk away from the whining child. If you're in the car or some other place where you can't walk

away from the youngster, invent a marvelous fantasy. Become so engrossed in it that you're not tempted to respond to the whining.

Give yourself a larger reward when you have reached your predetermined goal of not responding at all to whining. Treat yourself to a dinner out or a new suit.

3. Reinforce behaviors incompatible with whining. Let's say you're on an extended automobile trip. Your youngster is constantly complaining of thirst and is asking, "When will we get there?" at the rate of nineteen times every five minutes. Sing some songs with him (it's hard to whine and sing at the same time); if the youngster elects not to sing, at least you won't be able to hear the complaints. Start a search for out-of-state license plates. Make the game into a contest. The first person who spots twelve out-of-state plates gets to order whatever he wants when you stop for a snack.

Excessive Crying

Crying and children go together. Some youngsters cry more than others, as thresholds of pain and frustration vary a good deal in children. Excessive crying is crying designed (consciously or unconsciously) to elicit adult attention and sympathy.

The goal for remedying a problem like this is not to eliminate crying—there's nothing wrong with an honest expression of emotions—or to mask hurts. Rather, the goal is to give vent to hurt in a more moderate fashion.

Reinforcing a child for stopping his crying at an appropriate time is one way to help a child in this area. Let's take five-year-old Robbie as an example. Robbie was forever getting hurt. When he wasn't falling off his bike, he was getting hit by a ball or tumbling down the stairs.

When he was younger, the babysitter had comforted him after any mishaps. She had comforted him so well, in fact, that tears would flow from Robbie for the most minor scratches, and way past the point of the pain that had caused the tears.

His parents decided to reinforce the stopping of his crying at an appropriate point. When Robbie was stung by a bee he cried, of course, and his mother comforted him and put vinegar over the sting. In the midst of his tears she asked him a totally unrelated question: What movie did he want to see Sunday afternoon? Robbie choked back his sobs to answer the question. His mother acknowledged his answer. She then praised him for being brave and strong about the hurt. She took a magic marker out of her purse and painted a purple heart over the wound with an inscription: "Robbie Braxton—wasp bite—August 25, 1976." She explained to him that purple hearts were given to soldiers for bravery and that she felt he was being brave and strong. She told him she was quite proud of him for stopping the crying so quickly. Robbie's expression was a curious mixture of puzzlement (no one had ever called him brave and strong before) and pride (he *had* stopped crying rather quickly).

The next day he hurt himself playing ball, and he cried vociferously. His mother had seen the incident and knew the injury was not bad. This time she didn't comfort him but reminded him how brave he had been the day before. She told him she thought he could be a lot braver now. Then she told him she had other things to attend to. Robbie cried, but when he saw that it brought no attention or sympathy, he soon stopped.

Little by little Robbie's tears became more proportionate to the hurt involved. His parents could have continued to pay lots of attention to his tears, and their son might have ended up a crybaby, going through life exaggerating his wounds and feeling sorry for himself. Or they could have deliberately ignored his hurt and given him the message, either explicitly or implicitly, that crying is for babies, thereby developing in him a sense of machismo or an imperviousness to pain and feelings. Instead they deliberately taught him that tears are appropriate when you're hurt, but that you're a lot better off trying to overcome a hurt than feeling sorry for yourself.

Argumentativeness

The earlier you start, the easier it is to help a child overcome argumentativeness. You can do your part by making your expectations reasonable and being firm with your yes's and no's. Walk away—politely—from arguments. If a child has no one to argue with, he or she will have to stop.

Let your child know how much you appreciate his sense of logic and his love of the spoken word and that you'll be happy to discuss the issue over the dinner table or while taking a walk, but that now you're busy and have to get on with your business. Let the consequences do your arguing for you when it comes to your child's completing chores on time or living with decisions she has made. The family council (discussed in Chapter 12) is a good time to listen to arguments and a proper place for her to plead her case. The two-minute rule discussed in that chapter is a good way to teach children to state their views succinctly. You can also count and reward reductions in argumentative behavior. Counting will let the child know what you consider to be an argument.

Rebelliousness

Children have to learn to follow rules, yours and other adults'. If the youngster is having difficulty, find out why—if you can—and do something about it. Is the pressure in school too much? Is the church service too long for a child? Is the babysitter more interested in TV programs than in minding the child?

When children persistently misbehave, parents and/or teachers often label the child disobedient, unruly or worse and throw up their hands. This kind of situation has to be reversed, and the faster the better. An effective means of doing this is through a point system that covers a lot of behaviors. The technique can be used with children of all ages.

A personal crisis was hitting the Kowalski family. The parents were on the verge of divorce, and so much energy was being devoted to the problem that the children were being neglected. The tension and arguments between the parents didn't help either. Peter, age six, went backwards fast. Complaints began to come in from the neighbors: he was knocking over garbage cans, throwing stones at the geese, and leaving the corral gates open so the horses could get out, among other things. The bus driver and the teacher complained too. Within the family he was also impossible.

His parents decided to unite, at least on helping Peter. They told him that regardless of what happened between them, they would always take care of him. They listened to his fears and were as supportive as possible. But they also told him that he would have to settle down and not take the problem out on others. To help him behave, they told him, they would set up a point system. The system covered the following categories:

Following morning routines
School behavior
Bus behavior
Reports from neighbors
Dinnertime routines
Putting away toys
Taking a bath
Going to bed on time

Information as to how well Peter did was obtained through direct observation, calls to neighbors, and notes from the teacher and the school bus driver. For each category in which no disruptive behavior occurred, Peter earned one point. He could earn fifty-two points each week. The points were redeemable for various items. His parents made up a menu with the following items on it:

Dinner out on Friday night: 40 points
Four games of catch: 15 points
A puppy: 250 points
Making brownies: 10 points
Climbing Monument Mountain on Saturday with Father: 30 points

They tallied up the points each night at bedtime and posted them on a big chart in the bedroom. Peter became aware of his behavior and finally began to behave more appropriately.

This same system can be used with a teenager. Fourteen-year-old Cindy was going through an adolescent rebellion. Her grades fell. Often she didn't even attend school, and she was staying out past her curfew. In addition, her chores were being done sloppily, and she was being insolent to her parents. She herself wasn't happy about the conflicts she was having, but discussions (and especially admonitions) didn't help.

They set up a point system with her that covered the following areas: school attendance, chores, politeness toward parents, and curfew.

Each behavior counted as one point; a total of four points could be earned each school day, and three points on a weekend day. Three hundred points equaled permission (and money) to go on a youth hosteling trip, provided she passed all her subjects. The program started in December and ended in May. Cindy got permission to go on the trip.

Habits That May Trouble Parents: Thumb-sucking, Nail-biting, Carrying around Blankets, Stuffed Animals and Other Linus-like Props

Before you apply behavior modification to thumb-sucking, nail-biting or prop-carrying, ask why it is important to change the behavior. Whether the behavior is viewed negatively or positively, or not thought about at all, is usually as important as the behavior itself. There is nothing inherently wrong with thumb-sucking. It will not stunt a child's growth or cause any kind of psychological or physiological damage. Thus, you should consider whose needs would be met if thumb-sucking were stopped—yours or the child's. Does anyone have the right to impose his will on anyone else under such circumstances? Thumb-sucking might best be changed when the child himself or herself wants to change it.

Thumb-sucking

Thumb-sucking is usually more of a problem for parents than it is for a child—unless the child is subjected to ridicule for it. At one time thumb-sucking was looked upon as a sign of immaturity and even disturbance. Today we know better. It is a habit that some children develop because it feels good to them. But the habit often becomes entrenched because it becomes the focus of a power struggle.

If it is ignored, thumb-sucking usually goes away by itself. Parents therefore have to talk to grandparents, brothers and sisters, and other people who reinforce the thumb-sucking by calling so much negative attention to it. If you think it important to help the child get rid of thumb-sucking, use reinforcement of incompatible behavior; that will be a lot more effective than punishment. Time-out from positive reinforcement can be effective in treating thumb-sucking, but even that procedure should be used as a last resort.

Let's take the case of Richard. Richard was nine and a half; he had been sucking his thumb since he was less than a year old. Over a period of years his parents had scolded and fought with him over the issue. With the help of a behavioral psychologist, they did the following things. (1) They spoke to Richard about why they were concerned about the thumb-sucking. They felt that it subjected him to ridicule. (2) They told him they would help him overcome his habit. They set the kitchen timer for thirty minutes. Every time the timer went off and he hadn't sucked his thumb, he was to receive one point. A point chart (which also served to evaluate the program) was pasted onto the refrigerator so that everyone in the family could see it. Richard and his parents made up a list of things that Richard wanted: it included a Cub Scout knife and a neckerchief. They also listed chores he could buy himself out of with points. Prices were then fixed for each item. Whenever Richard accumulated enough points, he could redeem them for one of the items on the list. His parents also taught him to set up a competing response to the thumb-sucking. Whenever he felt his hand getting close to his mouth, Richard was taught to clench his fist twenty times to remind himself not to suck his thumb. (3) They worked out an agreement that if Richard sucked his thumb while watching TV, his parents would shut off the set for thirty minutes. At the end of the thirty minutes he could resume his watching. Richard agreed to this because he wanted to get the reward for giving up thumb-sucking and he felt this would help him. (4) His parents said that if Richard sucked his thumb while he was talking to them, they would time him out of the conversation for two minutes. (5) Finally, they told him that if he had to suck his thumb, he could do it in the bedroom, but no one would interact with him during that time.

Within a month Richard had stopped sucking his thumb completely. He even told his parents he had stopped sucking his thumb when he went to sleep at night. It was hard for him at first, but he felt much more mature.

The same methods can be used with children who suck on blankets or toys or their tongues.

Nail-biting

To reduce nail-biting it is most effective to work with a child, not on him. If the child can say, "I would like to stop biting my nails," or words to that effect, you're both so much ahead of the game. If there is no intrinsic motivation, you will have to provide an incentive to get him to want to stop the habit. You have to consider how important it is to you—and why—to effect a change in that behavior.

The intervention might consist of the following steps. (1) Make the child aware that he is biting his nails. Have him describe exactly what he does—how his hand moves close to his face, and so forth. This is done in order to make the youngster realize when he is about to bite his nails. Then, when he senses his hand come close to his face, or his elbow rise, he is in a better position to stop himself. (2) It helps to find out where the undesired behavior is most likely to occur—in class or while watching TV or before an athletic contest. You might then want to discuss with your child what makes those situations tense, and to work with him or her to reduce the anxiety of those situations. (3) Teach the child to exercise a competing behavior, such as clenching fists or grasping a pencil tightly in an unobtrusive manner. Try to let the child come up with an alternative response that is socially inconspicuous and easily compatible with ongoing activities. (4) Set up a point system like the one described in the section on thumb-sucking. An evaluation system is inherent in points.

Putting lotions and medicines on the fingernails is all right *if the child agrees to it.* If you put it on as a punishment or a deterrent, against the child's will, the chances are the youngster will wash it off when he or she is out of your sight and bite the nails anyway.

Carrying around Blankets, Stuffed Animals and Other Props

Again, carrying around a blanket or stuffed animal is not a problem for a child if it's not a problem for the parent. To prevent it from becoming a problem for the child might mean stopping grandparents, brothers and sisters, and others from ridiculing the child. Children, when left alone, will usually give up these things themselves, certainly before they go to kindergarten. Sometimes they give up their comforter all at once; other times it's more gradual. They might want their favorite blanket to go to sleep with or to carry on special visits, but they will not take it to nursery school or use it in outdoor play.

If you decide, however, that it's important to have your child give these up, work with her to help her do so. A good first step is to plan with the child when she will give up the habit. Sometimes it's helpful to set up an exchange. Give the child something else instead, such as a stuffed animal that is rather cumbersome to carry around. You can also strike a deal with the child—she may carry her blanket or teddy bear around the house, but she may not take it outside. Or, she may have her blanket or teddy bear inside her room, but not in the rest of the house. You might even restrict the use of the prop to bedtimes.

You can also set up an explicit reinforcement system, as with thumb-sucking and nail-biting.

Nervous Tics

There are a lot of theories as to why tics (habit spasms such as repeated eye-blinking, throat-clearing, shoulder spasms or shrugs) develop. No one really knows for sure. Many preschool children develop tics, especially eye blinks, for no apparent reason. Most of them disappear without anyone's doing anything about them.

With preschool children, probably the best way to handle a tic is just to live through it, although that is not easy. Even with older children and adolescents, tics often come and go without any intervention. If you sense, however, that the habit is becoming ingrained and/or that the child wants to rid himself of the behavior, there are behavioral procedures that can be used.

First review with the child why it is best to get rid of the tic. Better yet, let the child list for you all the embarrassments and inconveniences the habit has caused. Try to create as much intrinsic motivation as possible. If necessary tie a reward to overcoming the habit. Then work with the youngster on how to rid himself of the habit.

Have the child become aware of when the behavior occurs and teach him what to do to prevent the tic from manifesting itself. This requires a careful analysis of what muscle groups are used to complete the tic and what muscle groups are antagonistic to it. For example, take clearing the throat. It is impossible to clear the throat and exhale at the same time. To help a child stop clearing his throat, teach him to exhale forcefully the moment he senses the throat-clearing begin. For head-shaking, instruct the child to lift his chin as high as he can. Have him stretch the neck muscles until his head is perfectly still. Have him practice exercising those muscles. If rapid eye-blinking is the problem, the child should force the eye to stay open as soon as he feels the tic coming. In the case of eyelash-plucking or hair-twirling, the child can be instructed to spread her fingers apart in an inconspicuous way.

Have the youngster practice the competing behavior twenty times each time he or she is about to engage in the tic. Thus, a child might exhale twenty times each time he was going to clear his throat, or tense his shoulders twenty times instead of shrugging his shoulders, or spread his fingers apart twenty times each time he was going to pluck his eyelashes.

Some psychologists have recommended that with younger children the parent help the child to spread the fingers and then relax them the first twenty times. If you use this approach, take care to phase out your manual assistance when the child performs the exercise correctly.

It is also important to give as much support as possible to the youngster during this time. Comment favorably and frequently on his efforts. Also let the child know that you have noticed his improved appearance. Make these comments casually, and at unexpected times. It's best not to overdo it, of course, but verbal support is important. Every once in a while if you notice a lapse on the child's part, it is all right to suggest that the youngster practice the competing response.

Evaluation can consist of a simple count of how many times you see the child engage in the behavior. Youngsters can also keep their own records. If the child is motivated to change, extrinsic reinforcement is not needed so much as awareness, the knowledge of how to change the behavior, and your support and approval. But special rewards help too.

If there are undue difficulties or if you have trouble figuring out competing muscle responses, it might be worthwhile to discuss the problem with a psychologist. Many tics of long-standing duration have been eliminated in a single session.

Self-scratching

Self-scratching can be treated the same way tics are dealt with. The best competing activity for self-scratching is clenching fists or grasping a pencil or other object very tightly and then loosening the pressure. Have the youngster practice this activity twenty times when she gets the urge to scratch. Don't neglect motivation.

Rocking and Other Self-stimulatory Behaviors

A lot of children rock. No one is quite sure why this behavior develops. We do know it can be increased or curtailed by consequences.

It's largely a question of finding what will motivate the child not to rock. Usually it takes a host of consequences to do that.

Linda Sue was five; she had rocked since she was an infant. It was beginning to drive her mother to distraction, particularly when she did it in the car. And that of course was when Linda Sue did it most often.

The parents used the following method. They set up a point system involving a ticket with the hours of the day written all along the edges. For every hour Linda Sue did not rock, her mother or father punched the ticket once. Each punch hole was worth two cents. The parents kept Linda Sue aware of her progress. At the end of the first hour she was told how well she had done. She was also told she could earn a punch hole at the end of the following hour for not rocking. At the end of each day she was taken by her father to the candystore, where she could turn in her ticket for candy and toys. Her father's presence also reinforced her progress.

Linda Sue was given extra reinforcement for not rocking in the car, since her mother wanted her especially to decrease the rocking there. She could earn two punch holes for every trip she took in the car without rocking.

Linda Sue was allowed to rock in the house, but she had to do it in a special chair in the corner of her room. She did not lose the reward if she rocked there, but she was cut off from all social contacts. If she rocked away from the chair, she lost her two cents for that hour. She was instructed to stretch her arms out as far as she could whenever she felt an urge to rock. It took over a month to cut the rocking down to acceptable limits. But within two months it had been eliminated entirely.

Some families have successfully added a time-out procedure to the point system. Every time a child rocks she is sent to a special chair where she sits by herself. If the child keeps on rocking or refuses to get into the chair, she is sent to her room alone for five minutes without any toys.

One of the pluses of a point system is that it contains a built-in evaluation record. Obviously, the more punches, the more successful the program, so if punches are not earned, the motivation may have to be increased, or one of the steps described on page 28 may have to be employed.

CHAPTER XII

Responsibility and Independence

A parent's responsibility to a child is to see to it that he or she becomes self-sufficient. The more a child can do for herself, the more self-assured she will feel. The more a child can do for herself, the easier it is for the parent.

You can train a child to be independent almost from birth. One way of doing this is to let a child take responsibility for his or her own actions. When an infant throws food, for example, clear his plate away. The youngster then learns that the parent takes away his plate when food is thrown. Allow your son to use the car only if he returns it with the same amount of gas that was left in it. When Susie wants to play outside and asks her mother to dress her, even though she already knows how to dress herself, Mother can let Susie make up her own mind: if she wants to go out to play, she has to dress herself; if she doesn't want to dress herself, she can't go outside.

Another principle to keep in mind is to have a child do for himself what he is capable of doing. Take a look at what you do in the house and for your children. What are they capable of doing that you do for them, and how can they contribute their proportionate share to the household?

Let's examine some specific areas where it is important for children to do things on their own. These include dressing, grooming, taking care of possessions, cooperating with the family, being on time, and budgeting money.

Dressing

Being able to dress and undress oneself is a major step toward independence, and one that parents can hasten along. In order to learn to dress independently, a child has to be able to follow simple directions, imitate simple actions, and coordinate his two hands. It requires patience and teaching skill on the part of the adult, for tying a shoe is really quite complex, and even taking off an undershirt is a major task. A parent can best help a child learn these skills by concentrating on one step at a time and reinforcing each step that has been learned.

Children learn best when they can see the results of their actions. It is therefore best to teach dressing skills "backwards." Let's take undressing. If you want to teach your youngster how to take off her undershirt, for example, do everything but the last step—taking the garment off the left wrist. Let her do that (with your guidance, if necessary, but only until she can do it on her own), and she will feel the thrill of accomplishment that goes with mastering any new learning. When she can do that successfully, have her remove the shirt from her left elbow and her wrist. Reward her lavishly with praise and hugs for these accomplishments. When she has mastered those two steps, let her take the garment off her left shoulder, elbow and wrist. The next step is removing the undershirt from around her head. The final step is taking the undershirt off the right arm. When she can do that, you can both be proud that she can at least partially undress herself.

With pants, the same "backwards" sequence is followed. Do everything for him except taking his pants off the left ankle, and reward him when he can do that step by himself. Next, teach him to take the pants off his right ankle and so forth. Then have him push the pants down from his calves and step out of the right pants leg and then the left. Then teach him to push his pants down from his waist to the thighs to the calves. The last step in the sequence should be unbuckling the belt or opening the button or unfastening the snap.

Don't rush through the steps; they take time to teach. And don't go on to the next step until the previous one has been learned. If you take the time to analyze all the steps involved in putting on or taking off a garment, you'll have little trouble knowing what to teach. If they've been taught properly, three- and four-year-olds should certainly be able to undress themselves.

The same "backwards" sequence is applied to dressing. Do everything but the last step for the child, such as buttoning a shirt or pulling pants up to the waist. (If you are using elasticized waistbands, which I recommend over snaps and buttons, you won't have to do this.) Then teach the child to pull her pants up from the crotch area to the waist. Then teach her how to pull up the pants from the calves to the thighs to the crotch to the waist. Save the first step, stepping into the pants, for last.

Tying shoes sometimes presents problems to parents and children. First have your youngster observe you as you tie his shoes. Talk about how important it is to be able to tie your own shoes so you don't have to depend on anyone. Then do everything but the last step—pulling the laces tight to make a bow. Make a big deal out of it when your youngster can do that. Let him continue to do that for a day or two. Then do everything but step two, pulling the loop through the opening and tightening the laces to make the bow. Let him know he is even more remarkable when he can do both those steps. Next comes putting one loop around the other loop, guiding it through the opening and pulling tight to make a bow. You can teach these steps to the child while the shoe is on his foot, or you can have the child practice with his shoe off as long as the heel is facing him. After shoe-tying has been mastered, motivate the child to keep on with that skill by refusing to do it for him.

Grooming and Self-care

By the time children are two years old, they should be ready to learn to brush their teeth and wash up. Use positive consequences by serving breakfast after they have washed up.

By the time a child has reached the age of nine or ten he should be capable of taking care of his own clothes. Children can be taught to wash and iron and mend their own clothes. You have to set aside some time for training, but you will end up saving a lot of time, and the child will feel better in the process.

Requiring a child to care for his own clothes also saves a lot of wear and tear. A child who has to do his or her own ironing and mending is less likely to throw clothes around than a child who has these things done for him or her.

It also helps to give a child a voice in clothes selection. If a child is too young to make responsible choices, let him or her aid in the selection of color, then move to choosing between two styles.

There are at least three ways you can use reinforcement techniques in the area of grooming and clothes. First, motivate the child to dress herself by not doing it for her. Second, compliment the child when appropriate. Third, buy the child clothes and/or take him or her places on a contingent basis. Let's say, for example, that a youngster wants to buy two different kinds of pants. You can let him know that when he demonstrates that he can take care of what he has, then you will get him more. Be specific about what taking care of clothes means. It could mean laying them out at night, putting them in the washing machine when necessary, ironing them, or hanging them up at night. Almost certainly it will mean changing from school clothes to play clothes. Set up specific criteria with him, and keep a record of what he does. Then get him more clothes when he shows he can take care of what he has. In addition, take him places when he shows he is able to dress neatly enough to go.

Taking Care of Possessions

One of the surest ways to see to it that your child will be able to care for her possessions is by teaching her at a young age to keep her toys and her room in order.

With preschoolers, an effective way to build the habit of putting things away is to tell the child that at the end of a play period you will prepare a favorite snack or read a story or go for a walk when he has put his toys away. At the beginning you will have to help him to learn where things go and to get some idea of standards. While you are putting things away, emphasize the reasons you are taking such care—so he can find things when he wants them, so he can keep his possessions in good order and repair, so he does not have to be dependent on anyone to find out what he has and where it is, and whatever else is important in this regard.

Don't permit a child to play with other toys until she has put away those she is finished with. Praise a child when she puts things away, and let her know how nice it is that she is keeping the house so neat.

When the child has learned how to put things away but dawdles past the point where it's tolerable to you, consider using negative, but logically related, consequences. Give the child a reasonable and explicit time period in which to clean up. If the child doesn't do her job, do it for her, but put the toys away for a few days and tell her why you're doing so.

It is important not to give a child an overabundance of things. *When* the child demonstrates that she can take care of what she already has, *then* she can get more. Let your child know how long her toys have to last.

Give the child an expensive or delicate toy on a trial basis. If the child cares for it, he can keep it in his room and use it when he wants. If you find parts around the house or see that it is being misused, take it away and tell him he can use it only when it is convenient for you. That will motivate him to be more responsible with the toy.

Having a child earn toys and games is another way to get a youngster to value and care for possessions. When he has completed a chore, for instance, then he can get the skateboard. Children also have to be taught how to repair things. Set aside time to show them how to make repairs and a place where they can make them. What most parents find hardest is to let a child make repairs herself once she knows how to do it.

Another effective strategy for teaching care of possessions involves using a special box. This box can be for one room—the living room or family room, for example—or the whole house. Any time an article is left around and the owner is not there to put it away, it goes into the box. The box is opened once a week, and the owner gets his or her things back at that time. When a person has to go without her favorite shoes or sweater or game for a week, she is likely to begin to care more for her possessions and for the house. It's only fair to include yourself in this routine, so if necessary change your own habits so they are more in conformity with what you want to teach the youngsters.

Some people have effectively combined tying a reward to a reduction in the number of items left around with putting the items away for one-week periods. This usually speeds up the result, since there is a positive consequence as well as a negative one.

With the special box there is seldom a need for a formal evaluation system. If there is a reward tied to a reduction in the number of items left around, simply count the items or the number of times the room is left neat.

Cooperating with the Family

Family Meetings

The idea of a family meeting is to work together to resolve conflicts and to clarify responsibilities. The family meeting affords an excellent opportunity to show children how to be fair in the division of labor and free time.

Keeping communication open is the key to resolving differences. Except in emergencies, suggestions are more effective than commands. "Would it be better if——" teaches a child more than telling her what to do. It leads the child to weigh the pros and cons of situations and gives her the opportunity to exercise choice and accept responsibility for the decisions she makes. Choice is always better than coercion in this regard. If you strive for fairness and openness, issues do not have to be blown out of proportion. If you are patient and positive, even the thorniest issue can be resolved.

The following rules have been found to be helpful in running family meetings:

1. Schedule meetings at a regular time.
2. Any topic can be discussed, but each person has the right to temporarily refuse to discuss an issue.
3. No one can interrupt the person who is talking, but no one person can talk for longer than two minutes. In that way the more vociferous members of the family cannot monopolize the discussion.
4. Shouting is forbidden, as are judgmental statements such as "You're lazy," "You never care about anyone but yourself," "You never like anything."
5. Family members must talk directly to each other. Mother should not be expected to relay Mark's message to Father. Mother doesn't need that role, and if Mark wants to communicate with Father, he should do so directly.

Among the typical problems that come up in family council meetings are privacy, family members not getting along with each other, who brings guests over and when, whether or not a person is pulling his weight in the house, establishing fair systems for the use of the phone and TV, standards of dress and cleanliness, how much an allowance should be, radio and TV volume, where to spend a vacation, whether or not another cat should be accepted into the family, and who pays the fine on the library book that Jimmy borrowed but Susie didn't return.

In the family council be sure to differentiate between policy decisions—which belong solely to parents—and decisions that have to be worked out. An example of a policy matter might be a bedtime. Jimmy at age seven wants to go to bed at eight o'clock instead of seven-thirty. Someone has to draw the line somewhere, and if you feel he should be in bed at seven-thirty, it is your responsibility to stick to your guns. He can always earn a later bedtime later on. After you've listened to your teenager tell you why she needs the car, make a decision based on your judgment, and stick to it. You are the parent, and it's your car. Families need leaders sometimes.

Family meetings are also places where children and parents can ask for and receive help and encouragement for their dreams and aspirations. If Mother says she wants to go back to school, the rest of the family can encourage her with words and make it possible by deeds. The deeds in this case would be redistributing chores and resources so her dreams can come true. If five-year-old Samantha announces she wants to be a firewoman, her parents, brothers and sisters can help her by taking her to the firehouse so she can get a firsthand look at firefighters and how they live and what they do.

Family meetings are also places where social skills can be learned. If Johnny says he wants to move because no one on the block likes him, he can be taught through role-playing and other techniques how to get along better with people, and the family can make a concerted effort to hold a cookout for the children in the neighborhood so Johnny can have some positive contacts with the children.

The more open and positive a family is, the easier it is to solve problems. It is crucial that problems not be allowed to fester. If they are dealt with immediately, they are that much easier to resolve. Most important of all, the family council allows a parent to set an example of how to resolve differences. When a child has learned to resolve differences peacefully, he or she has learned a lot.

Chores

Having children share in family chores helps them develop a sense of responsibility and lightens the parents' work load. It gives children a sense of importance and a feeling of being active participants in the family. There is no reason to shortchange anyone because of his or her sex. There are no jobs that cannot be done by children of either sex. One way you can divide up chores is to list everything that has to be done: the cooking, the cleaning (with all it entails), the yard work, the laundry, the shopping, going to the dump, and all the rest.

Let everyone pick one job he wants to do, and then have everyone keep on choosing until all the jobs people don't mind doing are spoken for. Then divide up the rest of the jobs with some kind of rotation system. A voluntary commitment is a lot easier to carry through than one that is imposed on you. Once the jobs have been divided up, make up a chart. Even very young children should participate in this. A chart for a family of five—a twelve-, a ten- and a four-year-old (David)—might look like this:

Cooking breakfast: M—John; T—Mary; W—John; Th—Mary; F—John; Sat—Mother; Sun—Father
Cooking lunch: Everyone makes his own sandwich (Mother makes David's lunch)
Cooking dinner: M—Mother; T—Father; W—Mother; Th—Father; F—eat out; Sat—John; Sun—Mary
Setting table: John
Washing dishes: Mother on days she doesn't cook; Father on days he doesn't cook
Taking care of the yard: John, except for fall clean-up, when everyone pitches in
Shoveling snow: Mary
Vacuuming: Mary (once a week on Saturdays)
Dusting: John (Monday, Wednesday and Friday)
Sweeping: Mary
Garbage: Father
Feeding the dog: David
Bringing in mail and newspaper: David
Bringing in toys from outside: David
Keeping tools in place: David

Getting family members to fulfill responsibilities is not always easy. Getting people to agree and specifying who does what by when are the first two steps. Tying reinforcements to the completion of tasks—no one leaves the kitchen until it is clean or turns on the TV until after chore time—can help it go more smoothly. Some families also tie an allowance to completing chores.

Being on Time

Respect for time is something that develops gradually and has to be cultivated. The child has to discover that there are usually positive consequences for being on time and negative consequences for not being on time. Within the house consequences can be tied to chores. When chores are completed on time, then the child may watch TV or go out to play. When the child dawdles, then he or she misses out on fun activities. It's almost always best not to hurry a child. If a child takes her time getting dressed to go out and play, tell her you'll meet her outside when she is ready. She'll get the point soon enough, and you will avoid a power struggle and the reinforcement of dependency and dawdling. If you have an appointment, start getting the child dressed early and wait in the car for her. If she hasn't finished by the time you leave, just take her and let her finish dressing in the car.

Schedules also help children to appreciate the value of time. There are natural consequences built into a schedule. Children have to learn that there is no payoff in being late for dinner. If they are late, they have to eat what is left over or wait for the next meal. You might have to do something to make the meals more attractive so a child will not want to miss them, but don't teach a child that people are around to serve her at her convenience.

You can also avoid a lot of struggles and reinforcement of bad habits if you let a child face the consequences of his own actions regarding waking up and getting out of the house. The child will live up to whatever expectation you set up.

In the Taylor family the parents took turns getting their daughter off to school. On the days the mother took over, there was no difficulty. She woke Theresa at seven-thirty and asked her what she wanted for breakfast. Then she went downstairs and started the meal and the morning routines. If Theresa wasn't down by eight-fifteen, her mother reminded her that the bus would be there in five minutes. Theresa was free to come downstairs and eat breakfast or not. She was also free to miss the school bus. The mother made it clear that in that case she would have to walk, and if she didn't want to eat breakfast before school, that was her decision. Theresa usually ate breakfast and always caught the bus on time.

On the mornings her father took over, on the other hand, he would have to call her three or four times, fight with her over being down for breakfast, and once in a while drive her to school because she had missed the bus.

Theresa lived up to the expectations of each of her parents. Mr. Taylor tried to shield Theresa from the consequences of her actions, and he was hurting himself and his daughter in the process. It was unpleasant for him, and Theresa didn't really like interacting with her father in that way either.

If you have difficulty avoiding nagging and arguing with your child, you will be much better off (and she will too) if you make breakfast the night before and place it where she can get it easily, buy her an alarm clock and show her how to use it, and stay in bed while she gets herself off to school.

Bedtime schedules, as stated before, have to be respected too. When a child goes to bed on time at nine o'clock, then he can keep that bedtime. If he is in bed by nine-thirty after a lot of arguments when his bedtime is really nine o'clock, he has to start to bed earlier. The TV goes off, the lights go out, and that is that. If the child complains that he didn't have time to take his bath or complete his homework, ignore him completely. He knows, and you know, that he should have started those jobs earlier. He will start earlier next time if you are firm about not giving in to his stalling tactics.

Teach children to respect their curfews too. Don't let latenesses slip by you. Just as little children will test the limits of their parents, so will teenagers.

In many ways, the more a child has to do with his time, the more he will respect time. Idleness or not having goals breeds a disrespect for time. Since there is so much of it, why hurry? It is only when a child is busy (and fulfilled) that time will take on much meaning.

Budgeting Money

One of the surest ways to foster independence is to teach children how to use money. Money is one of those things, like time, that people seldom have enough of. Children might as well learn early in life the value of money and how they can get the most out of it.

Probably the best way to teach children the value of money is to have them earn it. Allowances can be made conditional on working with the family to accomplish chores. When the child completes his chores, then he gets his allowance. Set a clear policy on allowances: what has to be done to earn them, and what they are expected to cover. Some parents buy children their school supplies and whatever they require and then give them a small allowance. Other parents give —better yet, let the child earn—a larger allowance, from which the child is expected to buy his own school supplies and most of the other things he needs. Either way is fine as long as it is clear to everyone concerned.

It makes the most sense to let a child spend her own allowance any way she wants, even if the parent thinks it's being done foolishly. And be sure you don't make up for your child's "foolishness" (more accurately, different taste and values) by buying him or her other things when the child runs out of money.

Children need toys and games and clothes and all kinds of things. Many of them should be bought outright by parents, but there's nothing wrong with letting a child participate in the purchases. They will value what they get that much more. Train them to ask themselves what is needed, how much it costs, and whether or not they can get a better value for their money.

Once a child is of school age, there are ways he or she can earn money. One way might be to take over a chore from a more affluent brother or sister or parent. Another might be to make his or her own lunch and keep the lunch money. Getting paper routes, shoveling snow, mowing grass and selling lemonade are all old and honorable pursuits—children can have fun and end up with some extra money besides. Some families make it a policy to try to keep money within the house by hiring their children to do jobs that they would pay other people to do.

One mother, a writer by trade, used a housekeeper twice a week. Her daughter was always pestering her for clothes. The mother said there were x dollars allotted for clothes, but she would be willing to try her daughter out on the heavy cleaning and pay her the standard wages. The daughter agreed; the mother was relieved of the heavy housecleaning, and the daughter was able to buy her clothes.

Teenagers have lots of energy, and channeling it into meaningful work can help youngsters gain experience, money, and the knowledge that they can satisfy their own needs without having to ask anyone for anything.

It is important to encourage your child to get what he wants by his own efforts. It would be better to increase a child's allowance and decrease the toy budget than the other way around. In the long run you will save money as well, since the child is more likely to know and buy what he wants than you are.

Encourage your child to decide what he wants and then wait a week before he goes through with the purchase. That will help him avoid the kind of impulse-buying that can play such havoc with anyone's budget.

You might also set up a savings account for a child to help him get into the habit of saving. It's often best to retain control of this account, though, until the child reaches his or her majority. Fourteen- and fifteen-year-olds can easily go off the deep end when it comes to savings accounts.

Library fines, broken windows and the like should be paid for out of the youngster's allowance—you should not step in. Even five- and six-year-olds can be required to contribute some of their money if they destroy property. In this way the concept of value begins to take shape.

You can also make use of fairs or other such big events to teach the value of money. Let the child know when the fair is coming and encourage him or her to earn some extra money for it. If you want to see to it that your children have some money in their pockets for this occasion, set up some jobs (not routine ones) around the house that they can work at. A school-age child might clean out the attic or the basement. A younger child might gather up kindling or scrub out the sinks and the tub.

Children can be taught responsibility and self-reliance at any age, but the earlier you instill in a youngster the habit of caring for himself, the easier it will be for you and for him later on. The ability to take care of oneself breeds feelings of competence, self-worth and dignity. It is a legacy a child will profit from all his life.

Afterword

You

A parent is a person too. You have your own way of doing things and your own definition of happiness and fulfillment. Some of your happiness and fulfillment come through being a parent. But no one can fill all his or her needs that way. Guiding one or more human beings through the formative years is an awesome responsibility, and it's hard to balance taking care of yourself and another person. But bear in mind that when you are happy, your job as a parent will be easier and more satisfying. There are some ways you can help yourself.

One thing you can do is set aside some time for yourself—not your children or your partner, just you. That could mean taking a course—either for the fun of it or because you need to learn more about zoology in order to become a veterinarian. It could mean having one hour a day absolutely free to do with as you please, or it could mean working full time. Although you must give due consideration to your responsibilities and the needs of others, it's your life. When you get some of the things you want in life, you'll be in a better position to give to your children—and parenting requires a lot of giving.

You can also lighten some of your responsibilities by sharing them with other people. Spouses, babysitters, older children, day-care centers, camps, nursery schools and after-school programs can provide rich experiences for children and free you at the same time. For a parent without a partner it's almost imperative to delegate responsibilities.

Someone can come to your house to watch a child, or you can send him to someone else's house. Cooperative arrangements can also be made with other parents for play groups and babysitting. There are no easy solutions to child care, but there can be creative ones.

Another way of being good to yourself is to play—sports, games or whatever. Children should not have a monopoly on play. You can also sometimes join your child in play. This does not mean you have to crawl around on the floor or begin a game of Monopoly if you don't feel like it; but many children's games and activities can be fun. "Let's pretend" games, such as playing dolls or hiding in the woods, can be exhilarating. So can playing ball, swimming, skiing and sleigh-riding. Playing with a child can serve a double purpose. Your presence in a game can bring you closer to your child, and it can be fun for you too. You'll also find you have more energy.

Parenthood should be fun as well as work. When you feel more relaxed about yourself and your children, you will be a better parent. That was the purpose of writing this book: to ease you over some of the rough spots of child-rearing so that you can more readily enjoy the good times. The methods outlined here will be used most effectively if used creatively—and with large doses of love, acceptance and respect. Loving and accepting a child for herself or himself—and accepting yourself as well—will go a long way toward successfully resolving the many problems of child-rearing. And everyone thrives on success—you as well as your child.

Bibliography

Becker, W. *Parents Are Teachers: A Child Management Program.* Champaign, Ill.: Research Press, 1971.

Becker, W., and Becker, J. *Successful Parenthood.* Chicago: Follett, 1974.

Bijou, S., and Baer, D. *Child Development.* New York: Appleton-Century-Crofts, 1961.

Dreikurs, R., with Soltz, V. *Children: The Challenge.* New York: Hawthorn Books, 1964.

Fensterheim, H. *Help without Psychoanalysis.* New York: Stein and Day, 1971.

Gardner, R. *Understanding Children.* New York: Jason Aronson, Inc., 1973.

Givner, A., and Graubard, P. *A Handbook of Behavior Modification for the Classroom.* New York: Holt, Rinehart and Winston, 1974.

Gray, F., Graubard, P., and Rosenberg, H. "Little Brother Is Changing You," *Psychology Today,* March 1974.

Ilg, F., and Ames, L. *Child Behavior.* New York: Harper and Row, 1955.

Kanfer, F., and Phillips, J. *Learning Foundations of Behavior Therapy.* New York: John Wiley and Sons, 1970.

Krumboltz, J., and Krumboltz, H. *Changing Children's Behavior.* Englewood Cliffs, N.J.: Prentice-Hall, 1972.

Levine, M., and Levine, J. *The Parents' Encyclopedia.* New York: Thomas Y. Crowell Co., 1973.

O'Leary, K., and Wilson, T. *Behavior Therapy: Application and Outcome.* Englewood Cliffs, N.J.: Prentice-Hall, 1975.

Ramp, E., and Semb, G. (eds.) *Behavior Analysis: Areas of Research and Application.* Englewood Cliffs, N.J.: Prentice-Hall, 1975.

Ross, A. *Psychological Disorders of Children.* New York: McGraw-Hill, 1974.

Thomas, A., Chess, S., and Birch, H. *Temperament and Behavior Disorders in Children.* New York: New York University Press, 1968.

Selected issues of *The Journal of Applied Behavior Analysis, Behavior Therapy and Experimental Psychiatry,* and *Psychology Today* were also used.

Index

Accidents, toilet-training, 81, 84, 85
Adolescents. *See* Teenagers
Agreements, written, 21–23
Allowances, 179, 181
Animals, fear of, 110, 113. *See also* Dogs
Anxiety
  relief of through relaxation, 45–49
  over tests, 130–31
Appropriate punishment, examples of, 41
Argumentativeness
  dealing with, 162–63
  tantrums versus, 153
Artificial reinforcers, 17
Athletics. *See* Physical exercise; Sports
Attention-getting, through food struggles, 63, 65–66
Azrin, Nathan H., 83

Babies, 56–62
  breast feeding of, 56–57
  feeding schedules for, 57–59
  introducing solid foods to, 59–60
  jealousy of, 143
  sleep schedules for, 92–93
  weaning of, 60–62
Babysitters, and shy children, 146
Balanced diet, 56, 74
Barbers, alleviating fear of, 109–10
Bathing, resistance to, 151
Bedtime, 93–94
  "another drink of water" problem at, 33–34
  giving a bottle at, 61
Bedwetting, 86–89
Behavior evaluation. *See* Evaluation of progress
Behavior identification. *See* Identification
Behavior modification, 1–8
  benefits of, 6–8
  defined, 2–6
  for parents, 43–54
Biting
  while breast feeding, 57
  of nails, 166–67
Bladder control training, 83–86
Blankets, carrying of, 167–68
Blowups, 53–54
Boredom
  combating of, 141
  punctuality and, 180
Bowel training, 78–83
Breast feeding, 56–57
Bribing, reinforcement versus, 17
Brothers. *See* Sibling interaction
Budgeting, 180–82

Care of possessions, 174–75
Cellars, fear of, 112
Charts
  for chores, 178
  for company manners, 159, 160
  to control getting out of bed at night, 95
  for nighttime training, 88
  of praise, 15–16
  for school problems, 122, 132
  for toilet training, 80
Checklists, 28–29
Chores, allocating responsibility for, 25, 41, 177–79
Class clowns, dealing with, 133–34
Cleaning-up problems, 14–15, 20–21
Closets, fear of, 112
Clothes, care of, 173–74
Clowns, dealing with, 133–34
Clubs, and shy children, 146
Communications center, function of, 23
Company manners, 158–60
Competence, fostering feelings of, 8
Competition, sibling, 142–43
Concepts, teaching of, 119
Conditioning devices. *See* Reinforcement
Consequences. *See* Natural consequences
Consistency, 24
  in use of word "no," 39
  in weaning of babies, 61
Contracts, 21–23
Cooperation, 139–41, 176–79
Crazes, dealing with, 35–56
Crying, 161–62

Day camps, and shy children, 146
Deafness, selective, 33
Death fears, 104
Delayed gratification, avoiding of, 20
Dentists, fear of, 108
Desensitization, 49–50, 54
Desirable behavior, increasing of, 9–29
  step one: identification, 9–13
  step two: intervention, 13–21
  step three: evaluation, 26–29
Detachment, in behavior identification, 11
Diaries, 50–51, 54
  food, 70
Diet, 56, 74. *See also* Eating
Discipline. *See* Punishment
Divorces, fear of, 104–05
Dogs
  fear of, 108–09, 112
  as protectors, 96–97
Dreams, 97
Dressing, independence in, 172–73
Drug therapy, for bedwetting, 89

E & B Press, 129
Eating, 55–76. *See also* Breast feeding; Weaning methods
  good habits in, 74–76
  independence in, 62–63
  of junk foods, 67
  schedules for, 57–59
  of solid foods, 59–60
  struggles over, 63–65
  unhealthy habits in, 65–67
  for weight gain, 72–74
  for weight loss, 67–72
Education. *See* School
Effective reinforcers, list of, 17–18
Encouragement. *See* Reinforcement
Evaluation of progress
  basics of, 3–6
  in decreasing undesirable behavior, 31
  in fear mastery, 15
  in increasing desirable behavior, 26–29
  in overcoming homework problems, 129
  in toilet training, 80, 82
Excessive crying, 161–62
Exercise. *See* Physical exercise; Sports

Fads, dealing with, 35–36
Fairness in punishment, 41
Fair-pairs
  defined, 12
  for parents, 44
Falling, fear of, 113
Family interaction, 13–14, 137–43
Fears, 100–16
  nighttime, 96–98
  overcoming of, 103–15

Fears—(Cont.)
preventing of, 102–03
sources of, 100–01
Fighting, 3–4, 140–42
Finicky eaters, 65–67
Food, as reinforcer, 18, 80. *See also* Eating
Food diary, 70
Food struggles, dealing with, 63–65
Foxx, Richard M., 83

Games
for overactive children, 147, 148
and sibling fights, 141
Goal behavior, 20–21, 26–27
Goal-oriented nature of behavior modification, 6
Goals
toilet-training, 80, 82
weight-gain, 72
weight-loss, 68
Grandma's Law. *See* When-then proposition
Gratification, timing of, 19–20
Grooming, independence in, 173–74
Guidelines
for dealing with fears, 105–06
for punishment, 41–42
for sleep-schedules, 92
Guilt feelings, parental, 54

Handicapped persons, fear of, 109
Harsh punishment, criteria for use of, 39–40
Homework problems, 125–30
Honesty, in family interactions, 138

Identification
basics of, 3, 4, 6
of desirable behavior, 9–13
with family, 139–41
of homework problems, 128
of undesirable behavior, 31
Idiosyncratic nature of reinforcers, 18–19
Idle threats, 53
Idleness, punctuality and, 180
Ignoring
of fears, 116
of tantrums, 150, 151
Ignoring—(Cont.)
of undesirable behavior, 33–36
of whining, 160
Imaginary creatures, fear of, 110–11
Imagination, use of to overcome fears, 110–13
Imitation. *See also* Modeling
of eating habits, 56, 74
of fears, 100–01
of vocabulary, 118
Immediacy, in reinforcement, 19–20
Inadequacy, parental feelings of, 54
Incentives. *See* Reinforcement
Inconsistency, 7. *See also* Consistency
Independence, in eating, 62–63. *See also* Responsibility and independence
Indifference. *See* Ignoring
Insects, fear of, 109
Instructions, following of, 119
Intangible reinforcers, 15
Intellectual preparation for school, 118–20
Intervention. *See also* Reinforcement
to decrease undesirable behavior, 31
to improve eating habits, 72
to increase desirable behavior, 13–21
to overcome fears, 106
with reinforcement, 3, 4, 6
to solve homework problems, 128–29
in toilet training, 80, 82

Jealousy, sibling, 142–43
Junk food, 67

Kübler-Ross, Elisabeth, 104

Lying, 153–54

Manners, 157–60
Material reinforcers, 16, 18
Misbehavior. *See also* Problem behavior; Undesirable behavior
effects of focusing on, 8
in schools, 131–34
Modeling. *See also* Imitation
importance of, 138–39
to increase desirable behavior, 24–26
to overcome fears, 106–08
to teach manners, 157, 158
in weight-loss programs, 70
Monitoring of eating patterns, 73–74

Nagging, parental, 43–44
Nail-biting, 166–67
Naps, 95
Natural consequences, use of, 32–33, 84–85
Natural reinforcers, 16
Nervous tics, 168–69
New foods, introducing of, 59
Newborns. *See* Babies
Nighttime fears, 96–98
Nighttime problems. *See* Sleep and nighttime problems
Nighttime training, 86–89
"No"
  saying of, 51–52, 74–75
  teaching meaning of, 38–39
Non-sexist attitudes, generating of, 25
Nursery schools, for shy children, 146

Objectivity, in problem behavior identification, 11
Overactive children, 124, 147–49
Overattention, parental, 63
Overeating, handling problems of, 65–72

Parental love, 7–8
Parental overattention, 63
Parents
  advice for, 183–84
  behavior modification for, 43–54
Parties, joint, 141
Physical exercise. *See also* Sports
  encouraging risk-taking in, 102–03
  in weight-loss programs, 68, 70–71
Physical punishment, criteria for use of, 39–40
Planned ignoring. *See* Ignoring
Point systems
  to deal with rebelliousness, 163–65
  to deal with tantrums, 152–53
  to eliminate thumb-sucking, 166
  to handle rocking behavior, 170
Politeness. *See* Manners; Respect
Poor grades, 123–24
Positive thinking, in problem behavior identification, 13
Possessions, care of, 174–75
Praise. *See* Reinforcement
Prevention of fears, 102–03
Privacy, 142
Privileges
  deprivation of, as punishment, 41
  as effective reinforcers, 17–18
  rotation of, 143
Problem behavior, identification of, 9–13. *See also* Misbehavior; Undesirable behavior
Professional consultations, 116
Project Closer Look, 136
Promises, following through on, 53
Public places, and shy children, 146
Punctuality problems, 4–5, 19, 179–80
Punishment, 37–42
  versus behavior modification, 7–8
  to deal with sleep problems, 95–96
  for lying, 154
  versus natural consequences, 32

Questions, asking and answering of, 120

Readiness
  bowel-training, 79
  for school, 121–23
Reading problems, 126, 128–29
Reading programs, remedial, 129–30
Reassurance, to overcome fears, 103–04
Rebelliousness, 163–65
Records. *See also* Charts; Checklists; Diaries
  of idle threats, 53
  of nighttime training, 88
  in programs for reluctant eaters, 64
  in programs to increase desirable behavior, 26–27
  of sibling fights, 141
  in weight-loss programs, 68–71
Red Toothbrush, The (film), 108
Reinforcement
  for bladder control training, 83–86
  for bowel training, 79, 82
  for care of possessions, 175
  to combat sibling jealousy, 143
  for completion of chores, 178–79
  for cooperative behavior, 139–41
  to deal with rocking behavior, 170
  to deal with school problems, 121–22, 124, 128–29, 132–34
  to deal with sleep problems, 95

Reinforcement—(Cont.)
to deal with test-anxiety, 131
to deal with whining, 160–61
defined, 2, 15
delivery of, 23
to eliminate eating of junk food, 67
to eliminate food struggles, 64–65
for good manners, 158
for grooming, 174
to handle tantrums, 151–53
to increase desirable behavior, 15–21
intervention with, 3, 4, 6
in introducing solid foods, 59
for nighttime training, 88, 89
for overcoming fears, 105, 106, 115
for parents, 43–45, 53
and planned ignoring, 34–36
versus punishment, 8
of risk-taking, 102–03
of self-feeding, 62
to stop excessive crying, 161–62
to stop sibling fights, 142
to suppress nervous tics, 169
to teach children to interact, 145
to teach dressing skills, 172
for underweight children, 72
in weight-loss programs, 68, 71–72
Relaxation, for parents, 45–49, 54
Reluctant eaters, 64
Remedial reading programs, 129–30
Respect, 11, 52, 138
Responsibility and independence, 171–82
in budgeting, 180–82
in care of possessions, 174–75
in dressing, 172–73
familial cooperation in, 176–79
in grooming and self-care, 173–74
punctuality and, 179–80
Rewards. *See* Reinforcement
Risk-taking, to prevent fears, 102–03
Rocking behavior, 169–70
Role-playing
to deal with school problems, 135
to overcome fears, 113–15
to teach company manners, 158, 160
Routines. *See also* Schedules
in bladder control training, 84–85
establishing of, 23–24
Royal Canadian Air Force Book of Exercises, 71
Rudeness, 157–60

Schedules. *See also* Routines
for feeding babies, 57–59
punctuality and, 179, 180
for sleeping, 92–93
School, 117–35
getting along with teachers in, 134–35
homework problems and, 125–30
intellectual preparation for, 118–20
lack of readiness for, 121–23
misbehavior in, 131–34
resistance to, 124–25
social preparation for, 120–21
special education in, 135–36
test-anxiety and, 130–31
underachievement and poor grades in, 123–24
Scratching, 169
Selection of reinforcers, 18–19
Selective deafness, 33
Self-care, independence in, 173–74
Self-demand schedules, 57
Self-disparaging remarks, handling of, 130
Self-feeding, 62–63
Self-scratching, 169
Self-stimulatory behavior, 169–70
Self-sufficiency. *See* Independence
Self-worth, fostering feelings of, 8
Sex play, 155–57
Shoe-tying, 173
Shy children, 124, 144–46
Sibling interaction, 140–43
Sisters. *See* Sibling interaction
Situational changes, to decrease undesirable behavior, 31, 36–37
Sleep and nighttime problems, 91–99. *See also* Bedtime
afternoon napping, 93–96
getting out of bed, 95–96
nighttime fears, 96–98
schedules to deal with, 92–93
waking up, 98–99
Snackers, dealing with, 65–67
Social preparation for school, 120–21
Social problems, 150–70
argumentativeness, 162–63

Social problems—(Cont.)
- excessive crying, 161–62
- lying, 153–54
- rebelliousness, 163–65
- rudeness, 157–60
- self-scratching and nervous tics, 168–69
- sex play, 155–57
- stealing, 154–55
- tantrums, 150–53
- thumb-sucking, nail-biting and carrying around blankets and stuffed animals, 165–68
- whining, 160–61

Socialization, 137–49
- outside the family, 144–49
- within the family, 137–43

Solid foods, introducing of, 59–60
Special education, 135–36
Sports. *See also* Physical exercise
- encouraging risk-taking in, 102–03
- fear of, 114–15

SQRRR method, 127
Stealing, 154–55
Stress. *See* Anxiety
Stuffed animals, carrying of, 167–68
Survey, question, read, review and recite method, 127

Table manners, 157
Tangible reinforcers, 15
Tantrums, 150–53
Target behavior. *See* Goal behavior
Task completion, problems of, 148–49
Teachers, getting along with, 134–35
Teenagers
- budgeting by, 181–82
- name-calling by, 139
- point system for, 164–65

Tension. *See* Anxiety
Test-anxiety, 130–31
Thought stopping, 51, 54
Threats, idle, 53
Three-step system. *See* Evaluation of progress; Identification; Intervention
Thumb-sucking, 61, 165–66
Tics, 168–69
Time. *See* Punctuality problems
Time-out, effectiveness of, 36–37
Toilet training, 77–90
- for bladder control, 83–86
- for bowel control, 78–83
- nighttime, 86–89

Toilet Training in Less Than a Day (Azrin and Foxx), 83
Tone of voice, 26, 39, 52
Toys, care of, 174–75

Underachievement, 123–24
Underweight children, 72–74
Undesirable behavior, decreasing of, 30–42
- by changing the situation, 31
- by ignoring the behavior, 33–36
- by punishment, 37–42
- by removing children from situations, 36–37
- by using natural consequences, 32–33

Varied diet, 56
Vocabulary, teaching of, 118–19
Voice. *See* Tone of voice

Waking-up time, 98–99
Water
- drinking of at bedtime, 33–34
- fear of, 109

Weaning methods, 60–62
Weight-loss programs, 68–72
When-then proposition (Grandma's Law), 2
- care of possessions and, 175
- food struggles and, 64–65
- increasing desirable behavior with, 14–15
- for parents, 44
- sleep problems and, 91
- in teaching concepts, 119

Whining, 160–61
Written agreements, 21–23